Christ and the Tao

Heup Young KIM

WIPF & STOCK · Eugene, Oregon

Wipf and Stock Publishers
199 W 8th Ave, Suite 3
Eugene, OR 97401

Christ and the Tao
By Kim, Heup Young
Copyright©2003 by Kim, Heup Young
ISBN 13: 978-1-59244-568-4
Publication date 11/4/2010
Previously published by Christian Conference of Asia, 2003

CONTENTS

Preface v

PART I. CHRIST AND THE TAO: CONFUCIAN-CHRISTIAN DIALOGUE

Chapter One. *Ch'eng* and *Agape*: Sincerity Meets Love 3
1. Introduction to Confucian-Christian Dialogue 3
2. *Ch'eng*: Confucian Sincerity 8
3. *Agape*: Christian Love 16
4. *Ch'eng* and *Agape*: Sincerity Meets Love 24
5. Jesus Christ as the Tao 31

Chapter Two. *Liang-chi* and *Humanitas Christi*:
Sage Meets Christ 41
1. *Liang-chih*: Inner Sage 42
2. *Humanitas Christi*: the Humanity of Christ 53
3. *Liang-chih* and *Humanitas Christi*: Sage Meets Christ......... 67
4. The Tao of Jesus Christ 76

Chapter Three. *Imago Dei* and *T'ien-ming*:
John Calvin Meets Yi T'oegye 89
1. Original Humanity: *Imago Dei* and *T'ien-ming* 90
2. Existential Humanity: Fallen Nature and Human Mind 95
3. The Restoration of Original Humanity: Sanctification
   and Self-cultivation 102
4. Ecological Vision of Reverence: *Pietas* Meets *Ching* 111

Part II. CHRIST AS THE TAO: EAST ASIAN CONSTRUCTIVE THEOLOGY

Chapter Four. Owning Up To Our Own Metaphors: A Christian
Journey in the Confucian Wilderness 123
1. A Journey in the Confucian Wilderness 123
2. Theology from the Korean Vantage Point 127
3. Owning Up To Our Own Metaphors: Towards a Theotao 131

Chapter Five. God as the Tao: Toward a Theo-tao 135
1. A Call for Macro-Paradigm Shift in Theology 135
2. The Ugŭmch'i Phenomenon 138
3. The Phenomenology of *Sin-ki (Shen-ch'i)* 142
4. A Tao of Asian Theology in the 21st Century 148

Chapter Six. Jesus Christ as the Tao: Toward a Christotao 155
1. A *Koan*: Christological Impasse 155
2. A Parable: Return of Fish 159
3. Tao: a New Root-Metaphor for Jesus Christ 164
4. Korean Quests for Christotao 166
5. Jesus Christ as the Theanthropocosmic Tao 170
6. The Coming of *Yin* Christ 173

Glossary of Chinese (Korean) Terms 183

Credits 185

Preface

This volume is a collection of six essays that I published in various journals over the past several years. They represent the early period of my theological journey into Christian faith as a Korean Christian or, more broadly, an East Asian Christian. These essays deal primarily with religio-cultural themes related to my existential situation.

I was born and raised in a conservative Korean Confucian literati family steeped in about one and half millennia of Confucianism. My family-clan has carefully maintained a genealogy that contains the records (names, marital relations, and short biographies) of all ancestors from the beginning and faithfully observed communal practices of filial piety, i.e., ancestor veneration. I was the first Christian convert in this family milieu. Consequently, my journey into Christian faith has not been smooth and easy but accompanied by many anguished conflicts with my traditional background. This situation became even worse by the improper theology of a "Christ against Culture" model (according to the typology of Richard Niebuhr) in which I was indoctrinated.

The most dramatic incident happened at the funeral of my beloved mother. Using my status as the eldest son, I influenced to perform her funeral in a Christian style instead of a traditional Confucian one. This act, of course, involved an evangelical motive to make use of this event as an opportunity to proclaim the Good News to my stubborn Confucian relatives in accordance with the evangelical teaching of a charismatic Korean Church I attended. However, the result was tragic. Most of my relatives did not take kindly to this break in tradition, found this act offensive, and even viewed as a betrayal of our faithful tradition. After the funeral, my eldest uncle, the most authoritative person in my clan, privately summoned me and said with a mournful face, "I don't care what kind of faith you believe. But I have *never* expected that you would be the one to break our impeccable tradition of more than a thousand years!" This comment struck my mind like a flash of lightning to question whether there is something wrong in the orientation of my new faith in relation to my own community and culture. This quandary led me to commit myself to the study of Christian theology. The essays here, after all, are some of my theological reflections in response to that experience.

This situation entailed taking the study of Confucianism as a theological task, and Confucian-Christian dialogue has become an important part of my theological enterprise. By the course of the study I have formulated two Confucian-Christian dialogues focused on the thoughts of four seminal thinkers. The first dialogue was between Karl Barth (1886-1968) and Wang Yang-ming (1472-1529). Barth is probably the most significant Protestant theologian in the last century, while for some Wang is also the most important Neo-Confucian thinker after Chu-hsi. The second dialogue was attempted between John Calvin (1509-64) and Yi T'oegye (1501-70) whose thoughts have contributed the greatest influences to both traditions in Korea. Korea is distinctive as simultaneously the most Confucianized and the most Christianized country. On the one hand, Calvinist theology has made the greatest impact on Korean Christianity, especially through Korean Presbyterian churches, the so-called miracle of 20th century Christian mission, whose membership is the largest not only among all Christian denominations in Korea but also among the Reformed churches in the world. On the other hand, T'oegye left, without question, the strongest legacy in the history of Korean Confucianism.

Three essays pertaining to these two dialogues were brought together in the first part under the title of "Christ and the Tao." Among these, first two chapters are related to the first dialogue, and the third one to the second dialogue. The first chapter, "*Ch'eng* and *Agape:* Sincerity Meets Love," compares two key notions of Confucianism and Christianity, *ch'eng* (sincerity) and *agape* (love), based on the thoughts of Wang and Barth.

Although the Christian notion of *agape* is generally compared with the Confucian notion of *jen* (benevolence), homologically, *agape* is more comparable to *ch'eng*. In the structure of Neo-Confucian (esp. Wang's) thought, *jen* conveys a more ontological nuance denoting the primordial human-to-human relationship, i.e., co-humanity or being-in-togetherness, in a remarkable parallelism with the Christian notion of the *imago Dei* (the image of God). Furthermore, both *ch'eng* and *agape* similarly refer to a practice or embodiment (*sincer-ing* and *lov-ing*) of this ontological humanity (*jen* and *imago Dei*) in a concrete context.

The second chapter, "*Liang-chih* and *Humanitas Christi*: Inner Sage Meets Christ," continues to compare two root metaphors of Wang's Confucian thought (confuciology) and Barth's theology, *liang-chih* (the Inner Sage) and *humanitas Christi* (the humanity of Christ) respectively. These two metaphors are the centers and hermeneutical principles of their entire thought. The two are very similar but with different nuances and foci. *Liang-chih* focuses on immanent transcendence, whereas *humanitas Christi* underscores historical transcendence. However, both Wang and Barth are congruent not only in viewing these root metaphors as the transcendent ground for attaining full humanity but also in emphasizing the unity of knowing and acting (theology and ethics) in this process of humanization (self-cultivation and sanctification).

The third chapter, "*Imago Dei* and *T'ien-ming*: John Calvin Meets Yi T'oegye," compares two central notions, *T'ien-ming* (the mandate of Heaven) and *imago Dei*, based on the anthropologies of T'oegye and Calvin. This comparison presents even more striking similarities in method and content within radical differences of these two contemporaneous figures in culture and tradition. They agree: Human beings are inseparably related to the transcendental ground of being (God and Heaven). Original humanity reflects like a mirror the goodness of the transcendent ground. The psychosomatic mind-and-heart is the primary locus of humanity. And reverence (*ching* and *pietas*) is more central than doctrines. In addition, I argue that this thick resemblance is a plausible reason behind the rapid growth of the Korean Presbyterian Church.

In this manner, on the one hand, the essays in Part I are related to the issues that arise in the encounter between Christianity and Confucianism, such as how similar or different the two traditions are, where they really meet each other, and how their dialogue can be done. On the other hand, the essays in Part II under the theme of "Christ as the Tao" deal with the issue of how East Asian Christians can understand their Christian faith properly in this specific context (so to speak, a constructive theology 'beyond dialogue'). In fact, Part I and II correspond with the two stages of doing East Asian theology. While the first stage involves a descriptive and comparative study between Christianity and indigenous traditions (Confucianism in this case), the second stage entails a normative and constructive theological engagement in this boundary situation. Symbolically, as their titles express, Part I refers to the meeting between Christ *and* the Tao, and Part II proposes an integration of Christian faith in terms of Christ *as* the Tao.

The second part also consists of three essays. Chapter Four, "Owning Up To Our Own Metaphors: A Christian Journey in the Confucian Wilderness," tells my experience at an art colony where the old Confucian environment still remains relatively intact, which illuminated the significance of understanding indigenous spiritualities and surrounding cultures. A blind application of Christian doctrines without a proper consideration of the context could cause serious and long-lasting damage to the church and society as a whole. Since this short essay describes the concrete context of my theology, it can be regarded as *an introduction* of this book, a good place to begin reading.

Chapter Five, "God as the Tao: Toward a Theo-Tao,"

contends that the dualism between the two root-metaphors of contemporary theologies, logos (theo-logy) and praxis (theo-praxis), is problematic. It further argues that an employment of the East Asian root-metaphor tao is an alternative (theo-tao). This alternative bestows new theological vista and insights that can be used as profound resources to construct a global theology in the 21st century. As a parable to evoke readers to leap into this new vista, this chapter also includes a fascinating essay of Kim Chi-ha, a famous Korean poet.

Chapter Six, "Jesus Christ as the Tao," continues to develop this insight of theo-tao into Christology. Whereas logos was that of the Greek philosophical World, tao is the root-metaphor of the East Asian ethico-religious World. As Greco-Roman Christians conceived Christ as the incarnate logos (christo-logy), hence, it is legitimate for East Asian Christians to grasp Christ as the Tao of life (christo-tao). In fact, this fusion of horizon with the surrounding culture is inevitable as long as Christian faith in Jesus Christ has something to do with the totality of people's lives. From this vantage point, Jesus Christ is understood as the Theanthropocosmic Tao, the Way of life (serendipitous cosmic trajectory) in the ultimate communion of God, humanity, and cosmos. Furthermore, it anticipates the "Coming of Yin Christ," the Great Return of the "Mystical-Prophetic Female" to remedy the problems and errors caused by the Yang Christianities.

Chapters in Part I turn out to be somewhat scholarly and technical, while those in Part II are relatively easy and perhaps more fun to read. Hence, it will be a good idea for readers who are unfamiliar with theology and Confucianism to begin with essays in part II. If they become interested in Confucian-Christian dialogue, they will move into the first part. These essays were not produced for a single cohesive volume but separately for different occasions. However, I tried to preserve their original content as much as possible except for some minor revisions. As a result there may be similar themes in more than one chapter. Essays in this book reveal the cultural location and some basic insights of my theology. Nevertheless, they represent only *a* way of doing theology in one's own particular context and with one's own cultural metaphor. I hope that this book will be a catalyst to evoke readers to venture into doing their own theology from their own vista by boldly employing their own metaphors in their own context.

Finally, this publication would not have been possible without the enduring encouragement of Dr. Jae-woong Ahn, General Secretary of the Christian Conference of Asia. I sincerely thank him and his staff for their generous support and excellent cooperation to make this book available to the world. Furthermore, I am greatly indebted to my colleague Ho-Hyun JANG, Professor of Graphic Design, Kangnam University, for his fine design for the cover of this book.

PART I

CHRIST AND THE TAO: CONFUCIAN-CHRISTIAN DIALOGUE

Chapter One

Ch'eng and *Agape*: Sincerity Meets Love

1. Introduction to Confucian-Christian Dialogue

Since Confucianism is an embedded cultural-linguistic matrix for East Asian people, doing East Asian theology entails a critical wrestling with this living tradition. East Asian Christians are compelled to thematize a Christian theology of Confucianism that calls forth Confucian-Christian dialogue. To facilitate the dialogue between two different religious persuasions, I start with three presuppositions: (1) Confucianism as an expression of a faith, (2) confuciology as a heuristic device for a Confucian-Christian dialogue, and (3) the ortho-praxis of radical humanization (self-cultivation and sanctification) as a point of contact between Confucianism and Christianity.

(1) Whether Confucianism is an articulation of a faith is a controversial issue. The term faith in this context has a much broader definition than the Christian one, i.e., the informed trust in the salvific person. Rather, faith is conceived as "genetically human" (W. C. Smith) and "a constitutive dimension" of human being that involves primarily orthopraxis (R. Panikkar).[1] If faith is defined as an integrated human attitude toward transcendence, Confucianism is a faith. Although Confucianism is no institutional and dogmatic religion, it has a dimension of "being religious" (W. S. Smith).[2] Being religious in the Confucian context means to be engaged in "ultimate self-transformation as a communal act and a faithful response to the transcendent."[3] Tu Wei-ming defined Confucianism as "a faith in the living person's authentic possibility for self-transcendence." Tu further postulated a Confucian soteriology

as "the full realization of the anthropocosmic reality inherent in our human nature."⁴

Furthermore, the point of departure for the Confucian enterprise is the establishment of the will (*li-chih*), as Confucius said in the Analects, "At fifteen, I set my heart on learning."⁵ *Li-chih*, a crucial notion of Wang Yang-ming (1472-1529), refers to an ethico-religious commitment to a fully integrated humanity that involves a fundamental determination and radical turn of the will, similar to the Christian notion of *metanoia* (repentance).⁶ Although partially analogous to the Kierkegaardian notion of qualitative change,⁷ *li-chih* does not signify an "either-or" leap in response to the revelation of the divine ("the wholly other"), but a "both-and" return to human subjectivity in immanent-transcendence.⁸ This conception is not totally different from the Christian notion of faith. For example, the mature Barth also understood that faith is not merely an either-or leap related to the passive justification, but, rather, a spontaneous human self-determination for subjectivity that entails the process of sanctification, continuous repentance and regeneration, corresponding to the gracious divine election.⁹ The point of departure for both Confucianism and Christianity is not so much a logically construed metaphysics or a philosophy of religion, as a full ethico-religious commitment for the integrated human subjectivity. For both of them, the starting point is rather an establishment of one's will on the orthopraxis of the communally informed *Tao* (the Way).

(2) Confuciology as a heuristic device for a Confucian-Christian dialogue. Theology articulates a critical and coherent reflection on a faith in the theistic paradigm (*fides quaerens intellectum*). I use the term confuciology to designate an analogous type of systematic discourse for a faith in the Confucian paradigm. Confuciology designates an interpretative explication of the Confucian faith in a specific context. This term needs two further clarifications. First, the term is not a Confucian counterpart to Christology. Although confuciology includes an interpretation of the teachings of Confucius, it does not mean a specific discourse on the person of Confucius in the

way that Christology exclusively involves the interpretation of the person and work of Jesus Christ. Second, I am fully aware that not only Taoism but also Confucianism has an inherent suspicion and aversion against systematic discourse, because such a deliberation inevitably violates the natural flow of *Tao* (*wu-wei*). However, I argue that it is necessarily a heuristic device for a dialogue with Christian theology. Without such an attempt of post-modern construction, a necessity Tu Wei-ming also proposed in terms of "the third epoch," Confucianism would be an easy prey to be swallowed up by scientifically armed, modern, heavy-duty theological systems.

In terms of George Lindbeck, confuciology is "to give a normative explication of the meaning" which Confucianism has for East Asian people as their cultural-linguistic matrix.[10] If theology is a thick description of the intratextuality of the Christian faith, confuciology is that of the Confucian faith. Confuciology describes intelligibly and thickly the stories of the Confucian ethico-religious persuasions within their own contexts. Analogous to theology (at least similar to Barthian-Reformed and liberation theologies), being secondary to the faith itself, confuciology explicates rule of the game for understanding the cultural-linguistic matrix. It prevents an eclectic and fragmentary reading whose dangerous decontexualization jeopardizes and violates the integrity and inner coherence of the Confucian intratextuality. Hence, confuciology is a protective device to tell Confucian stories authentically and thickly in their own structures. Then, a Confucian-Christian encounter can be examined appropriately in the relation of and in the dynamic interplay between confuciology and theology.

(3) The ortho-praxis of radical humanization (self-cultivation and sanctification respectively) as a point of contact. The focus of the Confucian project lies in self-cultivation, learning how to be fully human, or an integrated attempt to realize human's intrinsic transcendental goal, "the achievement of a *radical* human-ity."[11] The point of departure of Confucian discourse is the concrete human situation of the living person

here and now. As its crucial notion propriety (*li*) denotes, its main concern is a person's proper embodiment of the *Tao* to a given ethico-religious context. Similarly to liberation theology, its prime locus is the shared orthopraxis of spirituality for its fundamental vision. Their visions are different: While liberation theology envisions an emancipatory spirituality for the fully shared society, confuciology embodies a sapiential spirituality for the anthropocosmic vision. However, both of them are a spirituality of the radical humanization of a living community here and now.

Also, theology underscores the issue of radical humanization; as Hans Küng puts it, being a Christian means being radically human.[12] Protestant theologies understand this as a theme of sanctification, a corresponding human action to the gracious election to achieve the full humanity that was realized once and for all for the human race through the redemptive life-act of Jesus Christ. Reformed theology, particularly that of Barth, emphasized sanctification as a central doctrine (equal in value to justification), following Calvin's shift of Gospel over law. Sanctification and justification are two expressions of an inseparable action of cosmic reconciliation. While justification is that from above, sanctification is the perspective from below.

My point at this juncture is twofold. First, radical humanization is a common issue of confuciology and theology (self-cultivation and sanctification), and this point of contact constitutes an appropriate locus to facilitate a Confucian-Christian dialogue. Secondly, the nature of this point of contact is primarily not a static concept or a psychological consciousness but a living person's dynamic engagement with a shared practice. The basic locus of the dialogue should be not a metaphysics, a psychology, or a philosophy of religion, though they are constitutive, but a spirituality of radical humanization. For their point of contact as well as their common ground first and foremost refers to the spiritual orthopraxis, an ethico-religious embodiment of each faith in a historical context.

Both theology and confuciology articulate descriptively and normatively the fabrics and intratextualities of their cultural-linguistic matrices. A Confucian-Christian dialogue can be formulated as interplay of confuciology and theology. Descriptively, the interplay is more related to a secondary level, a reflective level to examine the practical encounter, than to a primary level. Normatively, the discourse elicits an *a posteriori* thematization of the ethico-religious and theological meaning for a community in the historic Confucian-Christian encounter. This enterprise, thus, consists in two stages: (1) a descriptive-comparative stage and (2) a normative-constructive stage.

Confuciology constitutes the main device for the first stage. Pointing out the methodological dangers of a simple juxtaposition of Confucian categories with those of other religions, Henry Rosemont, Jr., proposed a method of "a concept cluster," the formulation of a conceptual framework for a more appropriate process of decontextualization and recontexualization.[13] Partially agreeing with this method, the significance of the contextual consideration, the method of confucioloy involves the much wider scope of the historical horizon, a systematic explication of the Confucian intratextuality. Although it uses modern categories for the sake of communication, its purpose is to tell its story in its own categories, properly resisting impositions of other categorical schemes. Hence, this stage takes equivocity more seriously than univocity.[14]

In the second, normative-constructive stage, the locus is shifted to the concrete context; namely, East Asian churches, Christian communities in the historic collision of the two spiritual traditions. Those communities need a holistic articulation of the Christian faith in their given cultural-linguistic matrix, namely, Confucianism. Hence, this stage inevitably focuses on their univocities. However, the goal of finding those univocative dimensions is primarily toward an *a posteriori* articulation of the Christian faith in the context of the fusion of the two horizons, more concretely, the two powerful stories of radical humanization. This enterprise does not refer to an arbitrary deliberation of speculative comparison, but an imperative thematization of a Christian community for the wholistic understanding of their faith. However, the result will enhance the theology of the Christian community as a whole.

In this chapter, I will present a case study of this method. First, for the stage of descriptive-comparative study, I will briefly deal with two key confuciological and theological notions, *ch'eng* and *agape*, represented by two paradigmatic thinkers, Wang Yang-ming and Karl Barth. Secondly, for the normative-constructive stage, I will propose a new understanding of Jesus Christ for the East Asian Churches; namely, a Confucian (Sage) Christology.

2. *Ch'eng*: Confucian Sincerity

1) The Self-Directing *Tao*

Confucianism claims that humanity is the heavenly endowment. *The Doctrine of the Mean* (*Chung-yung*) said, "What Heaven imparts to human beings is called human nature."[15] The primordial unity between humanity and Heaven (an East Asian expression of transcendence) constitutes the Confucian faith in the innate possibility (or perfectibility) for human self-transcendence.

In the context of this anthropocosmic vision, Confucianism addresses the mission of humanity in the world. Basically, however, Confucianism is suspicious of metaphysical and cosmological abstractions. As Confucianism is also called the learning to be human, its focus is rather upon practical issues such as how to attain sagehood, the original humanity. Confucius tried to demythologize mythical cosmologies rampant in the ancient period of China and reformulate the Confucian values in the new life situation. Therefore, Confucius emphasized the virtue of propriety (*li*), the orthopraxis of Way (*Tao*).[16] The crucial issue of Confucianism is not to obtain knowledge for the sake of theory, but how to embody the wisdom of *Tao* into a shared practice.

Although subtle and hidden, *Tao* is already immanent in the original human nature. It is a self-directing spirituality that gives a sapiential direction in a specific context. Etymologically, it means a human head in movement. *Tao* does not signify a static concept but a dynamic human action in the right way. Herbert Fingarette said well: "*Tao* is a Way, a path, a road, and by common metaphorical extensions it becomes in ancient China the right Way of life, the Way of governing, the ideal Way of human existence, the Way of the cosmos, the generative-normative Way (pattern, path, course) of existence as such."[17] As Fingarette further clarified, the Confucian freedom in the direction of *Tao* does not mean a choice among many alternatives but a capacity to locate one's act within the orthopraxis of the *Tao,* namely *propriety (li).*[18] According to *The Doctrine of the Mean,*

> To follow our original nature is called *Tao. Tao* cannot be separated from us for a moment. Cultivating *Tao* is called education. What can be separated from is not *Tao.* Therefore the profound persons are cautious over what they do not see and apprehensive over what they do not hear. There is nothing more visible than what is hidden and nothing more manifest than what is subtle. Therefore the profound persons are watchful over themselves when they are alone.[19]

To attain the ultimate human existence (sagehood) in the anthropocosmic vision, this passage said, one should be able to penetrate and perceive the direction of *Tao* beyond its hiddenness and subtlety. The Confucian profound person is such a person who has developed the necessary skills of cautiousness and watchfulness over his or her anthropocentric proclivities through self-cultivation. These skills refer to two key notions of Neo-Confucianism; namely, *ching* (mindfulness) and *ch'eng* (sincerity).[20] Keum Jang Tae, a Korean Confucian scholar, delineated these terms:

> Mindfulness refers to an attitude of faith that attempts to attain the ultimate human existence through the purification and attention of the human mind-and-heart in its fullest self-awareness. Sincerity signifies a mystical experience that maintains and realizes one's unity with the

ultimate human existence. That is to say, while mindfulness capacitates a human being to encounter, the transcendent dimension of its ultimate existence, sincerity enables a person to realize the mysterious union with the ultimate existence.[21]

2) *Ch'eng* (Sincerity)

According to *The Doctrine of the Mean*, *ch'eng* (sincerity) capacitates a person to follow the direction of *Tao*.[22] Sincerity does not refer to an intentional deliberation but an effortless, natural execution (*wu-wei*) of the Way, as it ought to be. Sincerity is the way to attain the true self; that is to say, an appropriate positioning of the self in the direction of *Tao*. On a deeper level, sincerity entails the freedom and capability of the profound person to embody naturally the spark of *Tao* in ethico-religious praxis.

Sincerity makes a person actualize the nature of one's own humanity to the utmost in the fullest moral sensitivity.[23] Hence, sage is defined as the absolutely sincere person, capable of extending the task of self-realization to the cosmos as a whole through authenticating his or her true nature in the ontological unity with Heaven. Sincerity denotes both "the creative process by which the existence of things becomes possible, and the ground of being on which the things as they really are ultimately one."[24] It is the foundation of both self-realization and self-transformation. Sincerity empowers a person to fulfill the very definition of humanness as "a self-transforming and self-realizing agent."[25]

Focusing on this spirituality of humanness immanent in one's concrete self, the absolutely sincere person, the sage, participates in the universal transforming process of the cosmic creativity. This implies the vertical dimension of the Confucian concrete-universal approach. As the Mencian analogy of the sinking of a well implies: "the dee\per one goes into the ground of one's own being, the closer one gets to the spring of common humanity and the source of cosmic creativity."[26] Mencius said, "For one to give full realization to one's mind is for one to understand one's own nature, and one who knows one's own nature will know Heaven."[27] Tu Wei-ming articulated succinctly:

Self-realization, however, is not a process of individuation; it is primarily a course of universal communion. The more one sinks into the depth of one's being, the more he transcends his anthropological restriction. Underlining this paradox is the Confucian belief that the true nature of man [human being] and the real creativity of the cosmos are both "grounded" in *sincerity*. When one, through self-cultivation, becomes absolutely sincere, one is the most authentic man [human being] and simultaneously participates in the transforming and nourishing process of the cosmos. To do so is to fulfill one's human nature.[28]

3) *Jen*: The Confucian Paradigm of Humanity

The Confucian locus of the mindfulness (an attitude of faith) and the sincerity (a mystical experience) is *hsin*, the human mind-and-heart. *Hsin*, a principle concept of the East Asian thought since Mencius, can be hardly grasped with the Greek philosophical framework that distinguishes body and soul as well as emotion and reason. It is not only cognitive but also affective, and also conative. In the Mencian sense, *hsin* refers not merely to a psychology, epistemology, or physiology, but also to ontology of humanness. It is "an ontological basis for moral self-cultivation" which constitutes the morality and subjectivity of human life.[29]

Focusing on this intrinsic possibility for self-transcendence, Wang Yang-ming identified the mind-and-heart with *li* (principle), the formative and normative principle of *Tao* or built-in structure of the cosmic order.[30] Wang perceived the mind-and-heart as the human locus where "the embodiment of the Heavenly Principle" (*T'ien-li*) eventuates (CSL: 7). Since *li* is a Neo-Confucian expression of transcendence, Wang's claim of *hsin chi li* signifies a Neo-Confucian soteriological leap that authenticates the human capacity to realize sufficiently the anthropocosmic reality inherent in human nature; that is to say, an immanent-transcendence.[31]

The basic paradigm of humanity in the anthropocosmic vision is perceived by *jen* (benevolence), the cardinal Confucian virtue since Confucius. Etymologically, its Chinese character, composed of a graph that means human being and two strokes that mean two, denotes two human beings, or togetherness of human beings. Hence, *jen* is also translated as "co-humanity," co-human," or co-humanize."³² The Confucian anthropology grounds in the axiom that *jen* (humanity) is *jen* (co-humanity). Since the first word *jen* means the Chinese gender-neutral term for a human being (*homo*), the axiom signifies that humanity is benevolent co-humanity. The immanent-transcendent self-conceived in the everyday living situation does not mean a self-fulfilled, individual ego in the modern sense, but a communal self or the togetherness of a self as "a center of relationship."³³

Neo-Confucianism expands the notion of *jen* to the cosmic togetherness of the anthropocosmic vision. Chang Tsai describes poetically in the *Western Inscription*:

> Heaven is my father and Earth is my mother, and even such a small creature as I finds an intimate place in their midst.
> Therefore that which fills the universe I regard as my body and that which directs the universe I consider as my nature.
> All people are my brothers and sisters, and all things are my companions.³⁴

Wang ontologized this anthropocosmic togetherness further in his doctrine of the Oneness of All Things:

> The profound person regards Heaven, earth, and the myriads things as one body. Such a person regards the world as one family and the country as one person. As to those who make a cleavage between objects and distinguish between the self and others, they are small people. That the profound person can regard Heaven, Earth, and the myriads things as one body is not because one deliberately wants to do so, but because it is natural human nature of one's mind that one does so. (CSL: 272)

The profound person of *jen* perceives the ontology of his or her humanity in an organismic unity with Heaven, Earth, and the myriads things. This realization of oneself as a cosmic being-in-togetherness enables a person to the cosmic spiritual communion with utmost "spiritual sensitivity and loving care."[35] *Jen* as the paradigm of humanity implies not only a manifested structure of human subjectivity but also a spiritual medium through which reconciliatory communion are made possible.[36]

Wang predicated *jen* as the "clear character" (*ming-te*) and the "loving people" (*ch'in-min*),[37] the two root-metaphors of *The Great Learning*. In terms of the substance-function relationship, the clear character defines the substance (the ontological structure) of humanity as a cosmic being-in-togetherness, while the loving people predicate its function (an ethico-religious realization). The "loving people," the function of *jen*, necessitates serious sociopolitical implications, by dynamically recovering the original structure of humanity as a cosmic being-in-togetherness. This love is basically prereflective and spontaneous like the feeling of commiseration. Its execution should follow the order of this natural feeling of social relations, started from one's nearest shared praxis and extended to the remotest. *The Great Learning* specifies the order of establishing and enlarging human relatedness through the extending networks of self, the family, the society at large, and the world.[38] Wang also argues against an ideal concept of Mohist's universal love, because this concept, with a weak starting point, is vulnerable to the abuse of "leveling" natural affections and responsibilities.[39] This stipulates the horizontal dimension of the Confucian concrete-universal approach, a spiral movement of creative transformation from the particular to the universal, from the inner to the outer, and from selfhood to the cosmos.

4) *Liang-chih*: The Confucian Root-Paradigm

Wang's confuciology culminats in his doctrine of *chih liang-chih*, meaning the extension of the innate knowledge of the good. *Liang-chih* is Wang's term designating the innate faculty of the mind-and-hearts to discern the Heavenly Principle and know the good. It refers to the prereflective and spontaneous feeling like the primordial human feeling of "alarm and commiseration" -- one of the Mencian Four

Beginnings of morality--when one sees a child about to fall into a well.[40] *Liang-chih* is revelatory knowledge of the Heavenly Principle in human original consciousness, whose content is "true sincerity and commiseration."[41] It is the foundation of all knowledge and learning including the teachings of the Sage (CSL: 150). It is the inherent moral standard to judge right and wrong, "the true secret" of the Confucian project of self-cultivation (CSL: 193). Tu Wei-ming rendered *liang-chih* as "primordial awareness," that is "an innermost state of human perception wherein knowledge and action form a unity" or the "'humanity of the heart' [which] creates values of human understanding as it encounters the world."[42] Hence, according to Wang, the whole Confucian project of radical humanization centers on the hermeneutics of *liang-chih*.

Wang established firmly *liang-chih* as the hermeneutical principle for the Confucian enterprise. The Classics are valuable as paradigmatic records of the work of *liang-chih* in the historical context, while sages are worthy as living paradigms of "*liang-chih* in action."[43] The stories of sages only as its "passing shadow" illustrate the trajectory of *liang-chih*. Wang said: "The thousand sages are all passing shadows; *Liang-chih* alone is my teacher."[44] Wang demythologized not only the authority of Classics and sages but also even that of Confucius himself. He claimed that the true Confucian foundation lies not in the person and work of Confucius but in the revelatory action of *liang-chih* (the *kerygma* of *liang-chih*, if you will) in every one's mind-and-heart.[45] Wang's notion of *liang-chih* shows a strong egalitarianism. *Liang-chih* as the inner sage is naturally endowed in all people, whether a sage, worthy, or stupid. Every person has an innate power to become fully human through the extension of one's *liang-chih*.[46]

Rejecting the distinction of the Ch'eng-Chu school between human nature (*hsing*) and mind-and-heart (*hsin*), Wang identified *liang-chih* with *hsin*-in-itself (literally, the original substance of the mind-and-heart), the state of "the equilibrium before the feelings are aroused."[47] This state of *hsin*-in-itself transcends any existential, ontic distinction of before and after, equilibrium and harmony, inner and external, or activity and tranquility (CSL: 137). *Liang-chih* as the *hsin*-in-itself refers to a primordial, ontological state of a dynamic being-in-itself. It is so bright and transparent like the "shining mind" and the "bright mirror" to be identical with the Heavenly Principle.[48]

Furthermore, Wang equated *liang-chih*-in-itself to the Great Vacuity (*T'ai-hsü*), the ultimate source of creative transcendence. Like the Great Vacuity, *liang-chih*-in-itself is absolutely self-transcendent.[49] The self-transcendent *liang-chih* entails the creative spirit, which capacitates not only cosmic differentiations through permeating all things but also warrants them into the anthropocosmic identification. *Liang-chih* substantiates the cosmic unity among diversities and the cosmic interpenetration through the work of its *ch'i* (material force).[50] In other words, *liang-chih* is the foundation of achieving *jen*, humanity as a cosmic being-in-togetherness.

Liang-chih as *hsin*-in-itself is also the life giving true self, the "subjectivity" of radical humanity.[51] As "the innermost and indissoluble reality" of the human, it is both "a self-generative 'intellectual intuition'" to empower a person to perceive the Heavenly Principle and "a self-sufficient 'anthropocosmic feeling'" to commission one to fulfill the mission of *jen*, to be a cosmic being-in-togetherness.[52] *Liang-chih* as the intellectual intuition and the anthropocosmic feeling constitutes the most concrete-universal foundation for the Confucian faith. For the concrete, transcendent possibility sufficiently generates the imperative of its universal extension. Through an extension of *liang-chih* in the ever-enlarging circles of relatedness, the bewildering self at the loss of equilibrium and harmony in the differentiated world can return to its true self. This is the Confucian concrete-universal way that implies the necessary identification of one's subjectivity and the cosmic ontological reality (the Unity of All Things).[53] In Wang's confuciology, hence, the whole Confucian learning is summarized into the doctrine of *chih liang-chih*, the extension of the innate knowledge of the good.

The foundation of *jen* (benevolent humanity), the substance of the Confucian persuasion, is *liang-chih*, and *ai* (love), its function, is conceived as a process of *chih liang-chih*. *Liang-chih* as a built-in order of the Heavenly Principle also constitutes the root-paradigms of four other Confucian virtues. Wang said, "It [the order] is righteousness [*i*]. To follow this order is called propriety [*li*]. To understand this order is called wisdom [*chih*]. And to follow this order from beginning to end is called faithfulness [*hsin*]" CSL: 223).

In Wang's confuciology, we find a positive articulation of the Confucian principle of reciprocity (*shu*), the single thread that binds all Confucius' teachings together.[54] Confucius said the negative golden rule, "Do not do unto others what you would not want others to do unto you."[55] Wang's affirmation does not betray the Confucian perception of reciprocity "as the human way par excellence."[56] Rather, Wang warranted *liang-chih* as the self-transcendent source for a person to capacitate dynamically one's reciprocity into practice, not only in networks of human relatedness but also in the cosmic pool of ecological relationship. Wang's ontology of humanity as a cosmic being-in-togetherness presupposes reciprocity and mutuality among beings-in-encounter. Wang's doctrine of the Unity of All Things articulates the Confucian anthropocosmic vision that entails cosmic and ecological reciprocity. The original Confucian suggestion is not to propagate an evangelical faith of the religiously privileged by means of domination, coercion, or exploitation. On the contrary, the humble and modest principles of *jen* and reciprocity reject any "epistemological immodesty and moral *hubris*."[57]

3. *Agape*: Christian Love

1) Election and Sanctification

A most important Barth's theological paradigm shift is the reversal of the traditional sequence of law and Gospel to Gospel and law, radicalizing John Calvin's attempt.[58] Barth criticized that Luther's doctrine of law and Gospel ensues a "dualist peril" and "anthropological narrowness" because of its dialectical separation of the two modes of the Word of God. Instead, he overcame the duality by reversing the sequence to subordinate law to the Gospel. The Gospel does not reveal the ultimate reality of God's grace dualistically. Since law is the necessary form of the Gospel whose content is grace, it should be understood in the context of the Gospel. This reversal--the triumph of Grace--constitutes Barth's radical revisions of traditional dogmatics: in his new formulation, Christology precedes the doctrine of sin; and ethics (law) is subsumed under dogmatics (Gospel).

Barth's doctrine of election saliently presents the paradigm shift. The sum of the Gospel is God's gracious election of the human race as God's covenant partners. This loving attitude of God claims a corresponding human response toward God, that is sanctification. However, God's election as the Lord of covenant already empowered us to be and become fully human, as God's covenant partners. In other words, if God's covenantal election is the ontological human condition, sanctification is the necessary human enterprise to realize this ultimate reality. In this context, the essence of a human being is conceived as free self-determination in action. The meaning of being and becoming a Christian lies in the unified action of hearing (dogmatics) and doing (ethics). Hence, Barth included ethics as a part of dogmatics in each of the three major volumes of *Church Dogmatics*. In these deliberations, his focus shifts "from the commanding position of God to the commanded position of humanity," which constitutes his theology to make a strong political impact.[59] Sometimes, as Robert Palma noticed, Barth exercised even the freedom of a "bracketing off the theological dimension."[60] Barth "intermittently excludes the theological dimension" to ascribe what Hans Frei called Barth's "secular sensibility."[61]

From this vantage point, it can be arguable that Barth's real focus is upon sanctification. Since sanctification belongs to election in Barth's supralapsarianism, sanctification is prior to justification. Barth emphasized that Calvin, his main theological basis, was a theologian of sanctification. Furthermore, since only love, the virtue of sanctification, has its own hymn in the Bible, I Corinthian 13, he argues, it is more crucial than faith, the virtue of justification. He says that *agape* is the Christian way that embraces faith and hope.[62]

2) *Humanitas Christi*: The Christian Root-Paradigm[63]

Humanitas Christi: Barth conceived that the foundation of sanctification is the exaltation of Christ, metaphorically presented as the homecoming of the Son of Man in the parable of the prodigal son (Lk. 15:11-32).[64] Jesus Christ is both *vere Deus* (truly God) and *vere homo* (truly human). *Vere homo* refers to God's complete assumption of humanity. This *humanitas Christ* (the humanity of Christ) is the foundation of Christian anthropology. Christology, "the particular knowledge of the man Jesus Christ," offers the basis for understanding of theological anthropology, including sin and human condition (IV/2: 27).

Sanctification conceived in the context of the exaltation of the humanity of Christ does not mean destruction or an alteration of humanity. The doctrine of *humanitas Christi* is related to election, incarnation, and resurrection and ascension, a theology of glory grounded in a theology of the cross. Since the humanity of Christ, both the electing God and the elected humanity, is the root-paradigm of God's gracious election, it is the root-paradigm of sanctification. The incarnation (*assumptio carnis*) of Jesus, God's becoming and being of human existence in totality, signifies ultimately the exaltation of human essence to divine essence. The resurrection and ascension are an inseparable, revelatory and historical event in which the risen Christ manifests Himself as the ultimate foundation of sanctification.

Barth's understanding of *humanitas Christi* entails the threefold concrete-universal act of God. First, *humanitas Christi* was the concrete-universal manifestation of God's election of the human race. Second, the incarnation of the

Triune God in the particular person Jesus was the historical, and thus the most concrete, fulfillment of God's salvific love for the human race. Third, the event of resurrection and ascension of the particular humanity of Jesus has opened once and for all the ontological basis for the redemption of humankind, and thus has established the universal foundation for the exaltation of the human race. Through the humanity of Christ in these events of election, incarnation, and resurrection and ascension, God has accomplished God's gracious will to humanity as God's covenant partner. Hence, the humanity of Christ is the revelation of God's most concrete-universal way of including humanity in His intratrinitarian history that established the ontological space of human sanctification. *Humanitas Christi* is God's revelation for the most concrete-universal paradigm of humanity.

Royal Man Christology: The most concrete-universal humanity was manifested in the life-act of the royal man Jesus (traditionally, the kingly office). The royal man Jesus, as both the root-paradigm of radical humanity and a mode of God's being, exhibits a revolutionary attitude "in a preferential option for the poor" against the exploitative established order. His life-act is the history of the Word in unity with deed (the unity of speech and act), which was dramatically expressed in his miracle stories. The life-act of the royal man Jesus reveals the paradigm of the unity of being and becoming, knowing and acting, and theology and ethics par excellence.

The cross of Jesus, the final negativity, paradoxically, constitutes all-embracing positivities, the resurrection. The cross, the most concrete point of the Christian faith, opens the new aeon of universal actualities. This dangerous memory of the Crucified, the most concrete point of the Christian faith, points to the inseparable dangerous memory of the resurrection of the Crucified, the most universal point of the Christian faith.

3) *Imago Dei*: The Christian Paradigm of Humanity

The mature Barth gave up his early claim in his commentary on Romans, "God is everything and, humanity is nothing."[65]

The living God becomes the dialogical and ontological partner of human in God's "sovereign togetherness" with humanity; God's deity with "the character of humanity" includes our humanity.[66]

In the doctrine of creation, Barth formulated the paradigm of human as (1) real human being in relation to God (vertical), (2) humanity in relation to others (horizontal), and (3) the whole person in relation to self (selfhood).[67] First, analogously to Jesus Christ who is from, to, and with God, real human being is defined as a person with Jesus in the hearing of the Word of God, as a historical being in gratitude, and as subjectivity in pure spontaneity to the grace of God. Secondly, since Jesus is a human being with and for other human beings, a person is the cosmic being that exists absolutely with and for its fellow beings. In the paradigm of Jesus, humanity (*Menschlichkeit*) means a joyful co-humanity (*Mitmenschlichkeit*). This image of God, fulfilled in the *humanitas Christi*, signifies humanity as co-humanity, being-in-encounter, life-in-fellowship, or history-in-partnership. Analogous to inter-trinitarian co-existence, co-inherence, and reciprocity, humanity, as the image of God, means a plurality as being-in-togetherness or a being-with-others. Thirdly, Jesus Christ is the paradigm of the whole person in the unity of soul and body. The human nature of the whole person is constituted by an interconnected unity of creaturely life (soul) and creaturely being (body).

4) The Direction (*Weisung*) of the Holy Spirit[68]

Barth conceived the direction of the Son as the basis of sanctification. The exaltation of Jesus as the royal man is its objective basis. Since the history of Jesus includes the history of all humanity, there is an ontological connection between the being of Jesus and all other beings (expressed in the Johannine writings in terms of abiding). Since this ontological reality that is the basis of the power of our conversion and our freedom is concealed, we need to recognize this ontological dignity to be and become radically and really human. Being and becoming a Christian is based on the operative power of transition from

Jesus to us. This transitional power of being and becoming has characteristics of light, liberation, knowledge, peace, and life. The New Testament testifies that this power is the work of the Holy Spirit. The Holy Spirit authenticates and sanctifies human beings as really human, and to be really Christian means to be radically human. Three decisive historical factors are: the royal man is the controlling center, the community is the goal, and the power of transition links the royal man and the community. The Holy Spirit effects the transition from Jesus to human beings in the distinctive history of the Trinity that is history as partnership (God is never solitary, but always has a partner). The history between the Father and the Son culminates in the concrete history of the Holy Spirit. The Holy Spirit is the basis of the riddle of the servant and royal man Jesus in the dialectic between humiliation and exaltation. The dialectic is not a paradox, but the *doxa* of God in the trinitarian life, entailing the powerful Yes of resurrection over the No of the cross. The Holy Spirit calls forth our response of thankfulness and brings us real joy, underscoring the theologies of resurrection and glory. The Holy Spirit also gives direction (*Weisung*) with its twofold meaning, wisdom and way. *Weisung*, very similar to the Confucian notion of *Tao*, directs, corrects, and instructs us to a concrete and sapiential way (on the march, not static) to becoming radically human.

Further, sanctification is realized in the relationship between the Holy One and the saints. Often, *de facto* we have not grasped our transformation (sanctification and conversion) that *de jure* has been realized in the Holy One. Sanctification *de jure* has come to humanity as an *a priori*, as the ontological connection with the Holy One. However, it is achieved *de facto* by our participation in the Body of Christ. A Christian is defined as a disturbed sinner by this *Weisung* of the Holy One. By a critical, but totally free direction, sanctification entails discipleship, conversion, works, and the cross.

The commanding summons of Jesus to "follow me" binds persons to the One in practice, which demands simple obedience in response to the irruption of God's coming

Kingdom. Christian discipleship in the reign of God requires our resolute renunciation of possessions, honor or fame, fixed ideas, family, and the absoluteness of religion. Conversion means an awakening of human involvement in totality, and a movement in faith in the opposite direction, to new humanity (renovation). However, new humanity is still present with old humanity (*simul iustus et peccator*). Thus, like a falling out or a quarrel, conversion still finds the human existence in a twofold movement. It also entails social relationship with others. Conversion is a public matter, as a public person acts in the totality of his or her being. Sanctification also entails works in mutuality (God's praise of our works and our praise of God's works). We do good works in correspondence to God's good works, and participate in God's works as His co-workers. Finally, the cross, as the limit and goal of our sanctification, reveals the most concrete form of fellowship between Christ and Christians. It involves persecution, sharing in tension, and temptations. However, it implies neither self-sought sufferings, nor the end of our life, but our sanctification. The cross is penultimate and provisional, for its real goal is to bring human beings joy in the eschatological hope of the coming Kingdom of eternal life.

5) *Agape*, the Christian Love[69]

Barth understood Christian love as a total human self-giving, in correspondence with faith as the reception of the total self-giving of God. *Agape*, self-giving love, is the way and the act, distinguished from self-love (*eros*). Although both *agape* and *eros* are related to human nature, *agape*-love is in correspondence with real human nature, while *eros*-love is in contradiction. Vertically, *agape* fulfills and transcends real human being in proper relationship with God, but *eros* falls short of it. Horizontally, *agape* affirms and realizes radical humanity, but *eros* betrays or denies humanity (as co-humanity). Only through self-giving love (*agape*) can we liberate ourselves from the vicious circle of destructive self-love (*eros*).

The foundation of Christian love (*agape*) is faith in the self-giving love of God. Our love is a free action, but as a secondary love, responding to a primary love. God, who is love, forms the ultimate basis of love in His triune mode of being. Divine love, as the external work of God (*opus Dei ad extra*) as well as the basis of human love, is an electing, purifying, and creative love.

Although it is exclusively grounded in the love of God in the trinitarian mode of being, our own action of love is equally significant. The act of love is new, free, sacrificial, and joyful. It is not merely a prolongation of the divine love, but a fully human act in return. This act of love has twofold content: the love for God and Jesus (the first commandment) and the love for neighbors (the second commandment). First of all, Christians are those who love God and Jesus in the freedom of obedience to the command of Jesus "You shall love the Lord your God with all your heart, with all your soul, and with all your mind, and with all your strength." This vertical love for God is not a theonomistic conception, but involves a real human act in continual subjection to the command. Secondly and equally, Christian love is the love for others, according to the other command of Jesus "You shall love your neighbor as yourself." This second commandment is as indispensable as the first. This commandment does not imply an abstract universal love of humanity, but a differentiated love in shared praxis. Thus, proximity is an important factor for its concrete realization. It always begins with specific fellow-people in the context of salvation history. Neighbor, in the biblical sense, means a reciprocal witness on the horizontal plane.

There is no revelation of love without a gracious inter-relating among people. While, in the final analysis, the emphasis on particularity is practical and provisional, the circle of mutual love must be widened to universal extension. Therefore, Barth's conception of horizontal Christian love is congruent with the Confucian notion of the concrete-universal approach. Finally, Christian love is the culminating manner of Christian life. Love is not merely an effluence of God's own life, but a real and concrete human act. Love, as the greatest among the manners of Christian life (faith, love, and hope), alone counts, alone conquers, and alone endures. In the last sentence of the *Church Dogmatics* IV/2, Barth said that "*agape* is *the* Way" (IV/2: 840).

4. *Ch'eng* and *Agape*: Sincerity Meets Love

1) A Confucian Turn of Barth

Barth's focal shift from the commanding position of God to the commanded position of humanity (sanctification) through the reversal of Gospel and law resonates the Confucian focal turn to the ethico-religious practice (propriety) of self-cultivation from cosmological postulations. Barth's doctrine of God's universal election coincides with the Confucian understanding of humanity as a heavenly endowment. Despite their different predications, obviously from their different perspectives, both Barth and Confucianism suggest a high ontology of humanity. Whereas human's ontological possibility for self-transcendence is perceived as a heavenly endowment from the Confucian perspective from the below, it is conceived as an elected being from Barth's Christian perspective from the above.

From this vantage point, Barth's theology shows intriguing Confucian-likenesses. Particularly with Wang's confuciology, Barth's theology presents thick resemblances. Both Wang and Barth challenged the established interpretive paradigms and made crucial paradigm changes, revolutionizing their traditions. Their paradigm changes share two converging goals, (1) maintaining a unified foundation of faith, guarding against dualism and (2) dynamically opening up the possibility of human involvement in the process of realization. Wang's identification of mind-and-heart with principle (*hsin chi li*) is a radical plea for a return to the Mencian tradition that established the authentic foundation of Confucian persuasion in the mind-and-heart, correcting Chu Hsi' excessive emphasis of principle (*ko-wu*). Barth's reversal of Gospel and law establishes the unity of the two modes of the Word of God, overcoming the dualism of Luther's doctrine of God and the narrowness of his theological anthropology.

Whereas Wang thematized his doctrine of the unity of knowing and acting from the primordial non-dualism in the structure of mind-and-heart (*li-chih*), Barth developed his doctrine of the unity of theology and ethics from the doctrine of election as the sum of the Gospel (faith). Both of them held a positive vision of an ultimately transcendent reality (immanent-transcendence in Confucianism, Grace in the Christian term). Generally, while theology thematizes explicitly, placing this vision to the forefront (focusing on justification), confuciology brackets it off, placing it in the background (focusing on self-cultivation). However, both Wang and Barth lessened these differences. Wang constructed a dynamic confuciology of self-cultivation, further developing the *Chung-yung*-ian vision of Heavenly embodiment into human nature (*liang-chih*). Barth brought the doctrine of sanctification to the forefront, thematizing the Christian vision of God's gracious election of the human race.

Both Wang and Barth affirmed the ontological unity of the human. Both emphasize the unity of the inner and the outer of the whole person, the self-determined being. Both agree that true humanity embraces the unity of knowing and acting (in the Confucian sense) or hearing and doing (in the Christian sense), between ontological knowledge and ethical practice or between orthodoxy and orthopraxis. The unity so conceived constitutes both Wang's confuciology and Barth's theology to produce a most dynamic, radical social hermeneutics in their traditions. For both Wang and Barth, radical humanization does not mean merely individual piety, but a collective process as teamwork of community (communal acts) with serious socio-political involvements.

2) The Root Paradigm: *Liang-chih* and *humanitas Christi*

Liang-chih (the innate knowledge of the good), the foundation for self-cultivation, constitutes the center of Wang's confuciology. Likewise, *humanitas Christi* (the humanity of Christ), the foundation of sanctification, constitute the center of and Barth's theology. Both *liang-chih* and the humanity of Christ refer to radical humanity--full, real, authentic, and true human subjectivity--the root-paradigm for radical humanization. These two central notions of Wang and Barth provided salient points of convergence and divergence.

Some points of convergence: First, both Wang and Barth took these root-paradigms as the hermeneutical principle for understanding their texts and traditions. Whereas Wang's confuciology is *liang-chih*-centered, Barth's theology is Christ-centered. Second, Christ also can be understood as an innate knowledge of the good (*liang-chih*) for Christians in relation to sin and evil. The knowledge of Christ reveals specificities of sin, just as *liang-chih* illuminates those of evil. Third, they congruently affirm the inseparability of ontological knowledge and ethical practice. While *liang-chih* manifests the proto-paradigm of the unity of knowing and acting, the life-act of Christ reveals the historical paradigm par excellence of the unity of logos and ethos, theory and praxis, and theology and ethics. Fourth, both manifest the most concrete-universal. Jesus Christ, the true God and the true humanity, is the most concrete-universal of the Christian faith. *Liang-chih*, the immanent transcendence of the Heavenly Tao in the human mind-and-heart is the most concrete-universal of the Confucian faith. Fifth, both *liang-chih* and the humanity of Christ as the most concrete-universal are self-transcendent, life-giving human subjectivity (true self).

Some points of divergence: First, whereas *liang-chih* is based on the anthropocosmic vision of immanent-transcendence, the humanity of Christ is founded on a faith in the gracious election of God and salvation history.[70] Second, while Wang thematized *liang-chih* as the immanent transcendence of the Heavenly Principle in the human mind-

and-heart, Barth articulated the humanity of Christ as the historical and personal incarnation of the divine *logos*. Third, whereas *liang-chih* is viewed as inner sage or incarnate wisdom endowed in every person's mind-and-heart, Jesus of Nazareth, a historical person, is comprehended as the assumption of the flesh (*assumptio carnis*) of the Triune God and Christ, the messianic figure. Wang focused on immanent potentiality, while Barth emphasized historical revelation. If *liang-chih* is an *immanent-transcendence*, Christ is a *historico-transcendence*. Fourth, whereas confuciology primarily focuses on ontological identification (e.g., the unity of all things), theology concentrates relatively on existential differentiation (e.g., the problem of evil). Fifth, thus, confuciology is strong in its all-embracing, anthropocosmic-sapiential articulation and relatively weak in dealing with the historical-existential problems of the human predicament, suffering, and death: theology is strong in dealing with existential-historical problems, while falling easily into an exclusivism, fundamentalism, or historical anthropocentrism.

3) The Paradigm of Humanity as Co-Humanity: *jen* and *imago Dei*

Liang-chih and the humanity of Christ can be divided into two dimensions: vertical (transcendental) and horizontal (human-to-human). Vertically, they are divergent (roughly, immanent-transcendence versus historico-transcendence). Horizontally, however, they are congruent. The Confucian notion of *jen* and Barth's understanding of the image of God show remarkably a substantial point of convergence. Whereas the cardinal Confucian virtue, *jen*, is grasped as benevolent co-humanity, Barth understood *imago Dei*--the paradigm of humanity--as joyful *Mitmenschlichkeit*. Hence, both Barth and Confucianism arrived at the same conclusion that the ontological paradigm of humanity is benevolent or joyful co-humanity, being-with-others, or being-in-togetherness. They alike claim that humanity (*jen* or *Menschlichkeit*) means co-humanity (*jen* or *Mitmenschlichkeit*). Wang and Barth held a congruent understanding of what it means to be human: to be human means to realize a radical being-in-togetherness in one's totality in the unity of body and soul. Bracketing off the vertical dimensions, they are congruent: being a Confucian or a Christian means being radically human which in turn means being co-human. This congruence constitutes a concrete, material point of convergence beyond their structural resemblances.

However, their divergent emphases of the root-paradigm--immanence and historicality--also affect their further formulations. Whereas Wang extended the notion of togetherness to the cosmic dimension, Barth focused on the meaning of co-humanity within the historical dimension. In this encounter, on the one hand, the Christian historical consciousness would challenge Neo-Confucianism to move beyond an innocent dream of anthropocosmic vision. On the other hand, the Neo-Confucian understanding of human being as a cosmic being-in-togetherness would be a corrective to evoke theology to move beyond its captivity of anthropocentric understanding of historical process which, some say, is responsible for the present ecological crisis.

4) *Chih Liang-chih* and the Direction (*Weisung*) of the Holy Spirit

Wang and Barth articulated a similar method of radical humanization. Both self-cultivation and sanctification point to radical humanization according to their root-paradigms, *liang-chih* and Jesus Christ. Both Wang and Barth viewed these root-paradigms as radical subjectivity generating the spiritual power of our being and becoming radically, really, and fully human. Both agree that self-cultivation and sanctification are an enactment of radical subjectivity beyond the existentially dysfunctional state. However, their foci diverge. Whereas confuciology primarily looks into the human mind-and-heart, theology focuses on the sinful structure of human condition. While Wang emphasized the capacity of human effort through the sincerity of the will (immanent, internal power), Barth focused on the transforming power of the Holy Spirit (transcendent, external power). Hence, while Wang consummated the insights of self-cultivation in the precept of the "extension" of *liang-chih*, Barth articulated sanctification as a participation in Christ under the direction of the Holy Spirit.

Nevertheless, Barth's insight of the direction (*Weisung*) of the Holy Spirit resonates with the Confucian notion of *Tao* (the Way). Fingarette explained the *Tao*:

> Thus there is no *genuine* option: either one follows the Way or one fails. To take any other 'route' than the Way is not a genuine road but a failure through weakness to follow *the* route. Neither the doctrine nor the imagery allows for choice, if we mean by choice a selection, by virtue of the agent's powers, of one out of several equally real options....
>
> Put in more general terms, the task is not conceived as a choice but as the attempt to characterize some object right or not. The moral task is to make a proper classification, to locate an act within the scheme of *li* [propriety].[71]

Likewise, Barth said,

> He [the Holy Spirit] does not, therefore, make us an offer or give us a chance. . . [but] places us at once at a very definite point of departure, in a very definite freedom. . . The Holy Spirit does not create the ghosts of a man [human being] standing in decision, but the reality of man [human being] concerning whom decision has already been made. . . (IV/2: 840)

Further, the *Weisung* does not put us "at a point or in a position," but sets us "on the way, on the march" (IV/2: 376). This metaphorical language for a dynamic action in progress or process rather than a static status echoes the radical of Chinese character *Tao* that symbolizes a movement, process, or action. The Chinese word *Tao* is an outstanding linguistic rendition of what Barth had in mind when he plays with the German word *Weisung* that has a twofold meaning, way and wisdom. *Tao* designates precisely such a sapiential way of life to be and become really, radically, fully human. Furthermore, the Way--

Tao or *Weisung*--in both traditions primarily refers to the orthopraxis, salient in the notions of Confucian propriety and Christian discipleship. We see here a good case that a Confucian notion illuminates theological material.

5) *Ch'eng* (sincerity) and *Agape* (love)

While *jen* is the cardinal virtue of the Confucian *Tao*, *agape* is that of the Christian *Weisung*. However, since *jen* is a Confucian notion more related to the human nature, it is more comparable to the Christian notion of *imago Dei*. *Agape* refers to an existential fulfillment of the image of God in theology. In confuciology, *ch'eng* (sincerity) involves an existential effort to realize the transcendent humanity (*jen* or *liang-chih* for Wang). If a Christian disturbed sinner is called a *loving* "hearer and doer" of the message of Grace, a Confucian profound person is a *sincere* "digger" in the anthropocosmic vision. Hence, a comparison of *agape* (the Christian love) and *ch'eng* (the Confucian sincerity) uncover salient features of their differences and similarities.

Ch'eng and *agape* are based on different perspectives. Whereas *ch'eng* is based on the Confucian all-embracing anthropocosmic vision, *agape* is rooted in the divine-human covenantal relationship in the context of salvation history. While *ch'eng* focuses on an ontological dimension of humanity (as a self-realizing and self-transforming agent for the cosmic equilibrium and harmony), *agape* primarily refers to an existential dimension of humanity (as a self-giving and reconciling agent beyond the human predicament of alienation and separation). Hence, whereas *ch'eng* as the Confucian *Tao* is more ontological (sincerity), *agape* as the Christian *Tao* is more existential (loving).

Nevertheless, both *ch'eng* and *agape* refer to a realization of ontological reality into existential totality, or in other words, a transformation of existential ambiguity by the ontological reality. *Agape* converges with *ch'eng* in the claim of the inseparability of ontological knowledge and ethical action. *Ch'eng* and *agape* congruently point to the transcendent human subjectivity in the unity of being in becoming. Furthermore, similar to Confucianism, Barth advocated a concrete-universal approach for the horizontal execution of *agape*. According to Barth, the Christian love (*agape*) does not refer to the abstract notion of undifferentiated, universal love, but entails a concrete-universal realization of co-humanity through ever-expanding human relatedness, namely, through the channels of neighbors in the salvation history.

5. Jesus Christ as the Tao

In this normative-constructive stage, the focus is shifted to East Asian and East-Asian-American churches, Christian communities in the historic collision of the two spiritual traditions. These communities need a wholistic grasp of the Christian faith in their given cultural-linguistic matrix (Confucianism) beyond the dialogue. This need inevitably forces us to focus on univocities between theology and confuciology. The main task of this univocative moment, rather, lies in an *a posteriori* articulation of the normative Christian faith for a community in a historic collision and/or fusion of two hermeneutical horizons, the two powerful stories of radical humanization. Primarily, hence, the normative-constructive enterprise does not refer to an arbitrary deliberation of speculative comparison, but an imperative thematization of these Christian communities for the wholistic understanding of their faith. Nevertheless, its theological implication will not be limited merely to these communities. A Christian constructive theology of Confucianism so conceived can make profound contributions to the world Christian communities as a whole by enhancing and improving theological categories and understandings.

The discussed points of convergence between confuciology and theology may constitute feasible points of departure to thematize a Christian constructive theology of Confucianism. The center of Christian faith is Jesus Christ. Now, I will focus on the question of how East Asian Christians better understand the meaning of Jesus Christ in the Confucian-Christian context. Jesus Christ is without doubt the root-paradigm of humanity. If an East Asian Christian finds the unity of *jen* and *imago Dei* and of *ch'eng* and *agape* in Jesus Christ, then, thick resemblances between Confucianism and Christianity will be substantiated in a form of Christology. If an East Asian Christian apprehends Jesus Christ as the paradigm of the ultimately sincere humanity (Sage) who has authenticated, once and for all, the Confucian faith in humanity's intrinsic possibility of self-transcendence, then, the Confucian story enriches and illuminates the story of Jesus Christ. In Jesus Christ, a Confucian-Christian experiences that the two stories of radical humanization encountered, collided, and fused with each other. From this vantage point, I will suggest five ways to understand the reality and meaning of Jesus Christ: (1) Christ as the *Tao*, (2) Christ as the Sage, (3) Christ as the *Ch'eng* par excellence (the most concrete-universal), (4) Christ as the Unity of *Jen* and *agape*, and (5) Christ as the *liang-chih*.

1) Jesus Christ as the Tao

First of all, the *Tao* (the Way) of Jesus Christ is a more preferable term than Christology. Jesus called himself as the Way (*Tao* [John 14:6]). The Greek *hodos* (the Way, also meaning path, road, route, journey, march, etc.) was an original name of Christianity (see Act 9:2; 19:9; 22:4; 24:14, 22). Jürgen Moltmann was correct to avoid the term and instead use the title *The Way of Jesus Christ* in his book on Christology.[72] For the reason, he said, the way-metaphor "embodies the aspect of process," "makes us aware that every human christology is historically conditioned and limited," and involves "an invitation" to follow "christopraxis."[73] He further said, "I am trying to think of Christ no longer statically, as one person in two natures or as a historical personality. I am trying to grasp him dynamically, in the forward movement of God's history with the world."[74]

If Christ is conceived as the *Tao*, the Confucian insight of *Tao* can clarify and enrich even further than Moltmann's. Borrowing Fingarette's phrases, Jesus Christ as the *Tao* means "the right Way of life, the Way of governing, the ideal Way of human existence, the Way of the cosmos, the generative-normative Way (pattern, path, course) of existence as such."[75] The life-act of Jesus signifies the culmination of propriety (*li*) according to a self-directing orthopraxis of *Tao* that Moltmann appropriately called christopraxis.

The parallelism between *Tao* and Barth's notion of the *Weisung* of the Holy Spirit further illuminates the sapiential character of the self-directing *Tao*. The freedom of Christian discipleship in the christopraxis and the outpouring power of the Holy Spirit converge with the freedom of propriety (*li*) that does not mean a choice among alternatives but a capacity to take part freely in the orthopraxis of the *Tao*.

2) Jesus Christ as the Sage (Sage Christology)

To attain the freedom of the *Tao*, Confucianism advocates mindfulness (*ching*) and sincerity (*ch'eng*). In the humanity of Christ, the royal humanity, a Confucian-Christian finds a perfection of both mindfulness and sincerity. The humanity of Christ is the ultimate human existence that attained once and for all the attention and purification of the mind-and-heart in its fullest capacity of awareness. Jesus Christ, as both the true God and the true humanity, realized and maintained the ultimate human existence in the complete unity with the Heaven. Jesus Christ is, in every aspect, the perfecter of sincerity. His works were not intentional deliberations, but effortless, natural executions (*wu-wei*) of the *Tao,* as they ought to be. Further, a Christian profound person finds Jesus as the absolutely sincere person, the true sage, who manifested the very definition of humanness as a self-transforming and self-realizing agent. Furthermore, a Christian sincere person apprehends Jesus Christ as the Sage-King who has fulfilled the complete normalization of humanity, fully restored its original goodness, and perfected the goal of self-cultivation,"Sageliness Within, Kingliness Without."

3) Jesus Christ as the *Ch'eng* Par Excellence (the Most Concrete-Universal)

In Christ the Sage-King, a Confucian-Christian sees that the concrete-universal way of the *Tao* is extended to the fullest horizons. The Confucian story of the benevolent humanity is collided and fused with the Christian story of the gracious God. The anthropocosmic drama is further substantiated and retold in an anthropo-theistic theatre. Now, a Christian profound person grasps Jesus Christ as both the concrete-universal authentification of humanity in the anthropocosmic vision and the concrete-universal embodiment of the Triune God in the human history. The humanity of Christ is the concrete-universal action of God's gracious election for the human race. The incarnation of the Triune God in the particular person Jesus is the historical, and thus the most concrete, manifestation of God's salvific love for the human race. The most concrete point of the Christian faith is the dangerous memory of the Crucified One, while its most universal point is the dangerous memory of the risen Christ.

The life-act of Jesus the Sage-King, as the single foundation of Christian theology and ethics, radically manifested the unity of ontological knowledge and ethical action. It is the history of a Word in unity with deeds, as the proto-paradigm of 'human being as the doer of the Word.' In His life-act, there is no distinction between *logos* and *ethos*, or speaking and action. Such a unity of word and deed resembles the etymological connotation of the Chinese character, *ch'eng*.[76] In the life-act of Jesus the Sage-King, a Christian sincere person perceives the historical manifestation of the *ch'eng*-sincering par excellence. In the miracles of Christ, the person finds examples of the process of divine-human sincering in the cosmic history. In the event of His crucifixion and resurrection, the person discovers a consummation of the concrete-universal drama of divine-human sincering in the history of the Trinity with the world.

Hence, sincerity in a Confucian-Christian sense means a faith in Jesus Christ.

4) Jesus Christ as the Paradigm of Humanity in the Unity of *Jen* and *Agape*

Jesus Christ is a human being with and for other human beings. His life-act was the full manifestation of *imago Dei*, meaning co-humanity, being-in-togetherness, being-in-encounter, life and history-in-partnership. A Confucian-Christian fascinates with the remarkable parallelism in the notions of *image Dei* and *jen*. A Christian profound person discovers the root-paradigm of humanity (*jen*) in the humanity of Christ as the image of God. A Christian sincere person is challenged by Christ as the perfecter of *agape*, a radically affirmative attitude of love through a self-giving, an action culminated on the cross. However, the Christian attitude of self-giving agape-love is also challenged by the Confucian attitude of self-critical reciprocity. An excessive attitude of Christian love without a necessary self-reflection and humility entices an epistemological immodesty and an ethical hubris.[77]

Moreover, traditional western theologies tend to remain under the captivity of the anthropocentric interpretation of history. Grounding the unity of *jen* and *agape* on the humanity of Christ, a Confucian Christology can recover the epistemological humility and ethical modesty and overcome the anthropocentricism by ecological and cosmic implications of the anthropocosmic vision. Christ the Sage is envisioned as the root-paradigm of humanity as a cosmic reconciled being-in-togetherness. The Confucian model of reciprocity and mutuality in the anthropocosmic interaction fosters a liberation of humanity and nature from the western models of domination and exploitation.[78]

5) Jesus Christ as the Ultimate Embodiment of *Liang-chih*

Finally, a Confucian-Christian grasps that Jesus Christ, the divine-human *ch'eng*-sincering par excellence, is the historical and personal incarnation of immanent-transcendence in the human mind-and-heart. Manifesting the unity of *ch'eng* and *agape*, Jesus Christ is the ultimate embodiment of the innate knowledge of the good (*liang-chih*). Jesus Christ fully reveals the pure and good knowing which not only naturally discerns good and evil but also radically uncovers specificities of sin and evil and the misery of the human condition.

Further, a Christian profound person perceives that Jesus Christ as the root-paradigm of radical humanization is the historical consummation of *chih liang-chih*, the omega point of the extension of the *liang-chih*. In Jesus Christ, the true God and the true humanity, the ontological connection of Heaven, humanity, and all things has been fully reestablished, and the human subjectivity has been completely identified with the ontological reality (*T'ien-li*).

In a Confucian Christology, hence, the two concrete-universal stories of *ch'eng* and *agape* are fully encountered. A Confucian Christology elicits the two encountered stories to move beyond dialogue and to be transformed into a new wholistic story of inclusive human being, profound human subjectivity, the novel paradigm of radical humanity (radicalizing and theologizing the Confucian axiom "Sageliness Within, Kingliness Without") in a new context, the eschatologically anthropocosmic vision in the new aeon.

Notes

[1] See Wilfred Cantwell Smith, *Faith and Belief* (Princeton: Princeton University Press, 1979), 129-142; and Raymond Panikkar, "Faith--A Constitutive Dimension of Man," *Journal of Ecumenical Studies* 8 (1971), trans. Pheme Perkins, 223-254.

[2] W. C. Smith established a distinction between "religion" and "being religious." While religion signifies an institution distinguished by a set of dogma, being religious means "a spiritual self-identification of the living members of a community of faith" (Tu Wei-ming, *Confucian Thought: Selfhood as a Creative Transformation* [Albany: State University of New

York Press, 1985), 132). See Smith, *The Meaning and End of Religion* (Minneapolis: Fortress Press, 1991), 19-74.

[3] Tu Wei-ming, *Centrality and Commonality: An Essay on Confucian Religiousness*, rev. ed. (Albany: State University of New York Press, 1989), 94.

[4] Tu, *Confucian Thought*, 55. Also, Keum Jang Tae regards Confucianism as a faith and advocates for its systematic formulation; see his *Problems of Confucian Thought* (Seoul: Ryugang Publishing Co., 1990).

[5] Analects 2:4.

[6] See Tu Wei-ming, *Neo-Confucianism in Action: Wang Yang-ming's Youth (1472-1509)* (Berkeley: University of California Press, 1976), 142.

[7] For the comparison of *li-chih* and the qualitative change, see Tu, *Humanity and Self-Cultivation: Essays in Confucian Thought* (Berkeley: Asian Humanities Press, 1979), 89-90.

[8] For this distinction, see Tu, *Centrality*, 116-121.

[9] For this discussion, see my dissertation, Heup Young Kim, "Sanctification and Self-Cultivation: A Study of Karl Barth and Neo-Confucianism (Wang Yang-ming)" (Ph.D. dissert., Graduate Theological Union, 1992), 115-6, 135, 164, 221-3.

[10] George Lindbeck, *The Nature of Doctrine: Religion and Theology in a Postliberal Age* (Philadelphia: The Westminster Press, 1984), 113.

[11] Julia Ching, *Confucianism and Christianity: A Comparative Study* (Tokyo: Kodansha, 1977), 105.

[12] H. Küng, *On Being a Christian*, trans. by Edward Quinn (Garden City, New York: Double Day & Co., Inc., 1984), 555ff.

[13] See Henry Rosemont, Jr., "Why Take Rights Seriously," *Human Rights and the World's Religions*, ed. by Leroy S. Rouner (Notre Dame: University of Notre Dame Press, 1988), 168-9.

[14] For this distinction, see Lee H. Yearly, *Mencius and Aquinas: Theories of Virtue and Conceptions of Courage* (Albany: State University of New York Press, 1990), 188-191.

[15] For a translation, see Chan Wing-tsit, *A Source Book in Chinese Philosophy* (Princeton: Princeton University Press, 1963), 95. Modified.

[16] See Herbert Fingarette, *Confucius--the Secular as Sacred* (New York: Harper & Row, 1979), chap. 1.

[17] Ibid., 19.

[18] See ibid., 22.

[19] Chan, *Source Book*, 98. Modified.

[20] For *ching*, see Michael C. Kalton, *To Become A Sage: The Ten Diagrams on Sage Learning by Yi T'oegye* (New York: Columbia Press, 1988), 212-4. Whereas English word sincerity holds some negative

connotations, *ch'eng* always refers to positive meanings such as honesty, genuineness, and truth. Etymologically, *ch'eng* means the completion, actualization, and perfection of the words, or the unity of words and deeds.

[21] Keum Jang Tae, *Problems*, 11; also see 8-11. My translation.

[22] *The Doctrine of the Mean* said:
"Sincerity is the Way of Heaven. To think how to be sincere is the way of human being. One who is sincere is one who hits upon what is right without effort and apprehends without thinking. A person is naturally and easily in harmony with the Way. Such a person is a sage. One who tries to be sincere is one who chooses the good and holds fast to it." (Chan, *Source Book*, 107. Modified)

[23] *The Doctrine of the Means* said:
"Only those who are absolutely sincere can order and adjust the great relation of humankind, establish the great foundation of humanity, and know the transforming and nourishing operations of Heaven and Earth. Does a person depend on anything else? How earnest and sincere--a person is humanity! How deep and unfathomable--a person is abyss! How vast and great--a person is Heaven! Who can know the person except one who really has quickness of apprehension, intelligence, sageliness, and wisdom, and understand the character of Heaven?" (Chan, *Source Book*, 112. Modified)

[24] Tu Wei-ming, *Humanity and Self-Cultivation: Essays in Confucian Thought* (Berkeley: Asian Humanities Press, 1979), 97.

[25] Ibid.

[26] Tu, *Humanity*, 87-8.

[27] D. C. Lau, *Mencius* (Harmondsworth, England: Penguin Books, 1970), 182. Modified.

[28] Tu, *Humanity*, 99.

[29] Tu, *Confucian Thought*, 70.

[30] *Li* refers to a built-in structure, pattern, or standard that holds the order of universe as a whole. *Li* and *Tao* are generally same: *li* is more concrete whereas *Tao* is broader. Chan Wing-tsit, trans., *Instructions for Practical Living and Other Confucian Writings of Wang Yang-ming* (New York: Columbia University Press, 1963), 6-7. Abbreviation: CSL.

[31] For the notion of immanent transcendence, see Liu Shu-Hsien's article, "The Confucian Approach to the Problem of Transcendence and Immanence, " in *Philosophy East and West* 22 (1972), 45-52.

[32] See Peter A. Booderberg, "The Semasiology of Some Primary Confucian Concepts," *Philosophy East and West* 2:4 (1953), 329-30.

[33] Tu Wei-ming, *Centrality*, 53.

[34] Chan, *Source Book*, 497.

[35] Tu, *Humanity*, 157.

[36] See CSL: 272.
[37] Rejecting Chu Hsi's revision of this word to "renovating people" (*hsin-min*), Wang argued for this original rendition. See CSL: 276. For the passage of *The Great Learning*, see Chan, *Source Book*, 86.
[38] See CSL: 273-4.
[39] Ibid., 56-57.
[40] Mencius 2A:6. James Legge, *The Chinese Classics*, v. 2 (New York: Paragon Books, 1966), 78.
[41] CSL: 176. Also see Hitoyuki, "Wang Yang-ming's Doctrine of Innate Knowledge of the Good," *Philosophy East and West* 11 (1961), 41-2.
[42] Tu, *Confucian Thought*, 32.
[43] Philip Ivanhoe, *Ethics in the Confucian Tradition: The Thought of Mencius and Wang Yang-ming* (Atlanta: Scholars Press, 1990), 103. Also, see CSL: 23.
[44] Recited from Ivanhoe, 104.
[45] CSL: 159. Also see Ivanhoe, 109.
[46] See CSL: 194.
[47] CSL: 136.
[48] CSL: 139-140; 148-9; see 152.
[49] CSL: 220.
[50] CSL: 221-2.
[51] Tu, *Humanity*, 138-61; also CSL: 80-1.
[52] Tu, *Humanity*, 156.
[53] Ibid., 159.
[54] D. C. Lau, *Confucius: The Analects*, 74, 132.
[55] Ibid., 135.
[56] Tu, *Commonality*, 103.
[57] Robert E. Allison, "The Ethics of Confucianism and Christianity: The Delicate Balance," *Ching Feng* 33:3 (1990), 168.
[58] For Barth's reversal of Gospel and law, see Eberhard Jüngel's article, "Gospel and Law: The Relationship of Dogmatics and Ethics," in his *Karl Barth, a Theological Legacy*, trans. Garrett E. Paul (Philadelphia: The Westminster Press, 1986), 105-126.
[59] Jüngel, *Barth*, 126.
[60] See Karl J. Palma, *Karl Barth's Theology of Culture: The Freedom of Culture for the Praise of God* (Allison Park, PA: Pickwick Publications, 1983), 10-14.
[61] Ibid., 11 and 13; also Hans Frei, "Karl Barth--Theologian," in *Karl Barth and the Future of Theology*, ed. David L. Dickermann (New Haven: Yale Divinity School Association, 1969), 8-9.
[62] See Karl Barth, *Church Dogmatics, Vol. IV, Part II: The Doctrine of*

Reconciliation, trans. by G. W. Bromiley (Edinburgh: T. & T. Clark, 1958), 840. Abbreviation: IV/2.

⁶³ For this topic, see CD IV/2, Sec. 64. 2, 3; also, see Kim, "Sanctification and Self-cultivation," 125-138.

⁶⁴ IV/2, 21-25.

⁶⁵ Karl Barth, *The Epistle To the Romans*, 6th ed., trans. Edwyn C. Hoskyns (London: Oxford University Press, 1933).

⁶⁶ See Barth, *The Humanity of God*, trans. John Newton Thomas and Thomas Wieser (Atlanta: John Knox Press, 1960), 45f.

⁶⁷ Stuart D. McLean, *Humanity in the Thought of Karl Barth* (Edinburgh: T. & T. Clark, 1981); also CD III/2.

⁶⁸ See CD IV/2, Secs. 64.4 and 66; also Kim, "Sanctification and Self-cultivation," 158-182.

⁶⁹ For this topic, see CD IV/2, Sec. 68; also Kim, "Sanctification and Self-cultivation," 183-203.

⁷⁰ The election of God through the salvation history also has a dimension of immanent-transcendence. However, it basically grounds on the radical transcendence and focuses on its historical immanence.

⁷¹ Fingarette, *Confucius*, 21-2.

⁷² J. Moltmann, *The Way of Jesus Christ: Christology in Messianic Dimensions*, trans. by Magaret Kohl (San Francisco: Harper, 1990).

⁷³ Ibid., xiv.

⁷⁴ Ibid., xv.

⁷⁵ Ibid., 19.

⁷⁶ The Chinese character *ch'eng* consists of two graphs that mean word (or speech) and accomplishment (action); etymologically, it denotes sincere actualization of one's word. Hence, I also translate *ch'eng* in the gerund form "sincering" to emphasize its dynamic and active dimension.

⁷⁷ See Allison, 168.

⁷⁸ See Tu Wei-ming, *Centrality and Commonality: An Essay on Confucian Religiousness*, rev. ed. (Albany: State Univ. of New York Press, 1989), 102-107.

Chapter Two

Liang-chih and *Humanitas Christi:* Sage Meets Christ

Confucianism and Christianity are radically different religious persuasions that have emerged from distinct historical-cultural-social-linguistic contexts. If Christianity is a prophetic tradition based on the revealed Word of God, Confucianism is a sapiential tradition based on the human mind-and-heart. However, such a distinction of comparative religion is not sufficient for Korean Christians. For Confucianism is an unavoidably given tradition that still remains as a living cultural-linguistic matrix embedded in our mind-and-heart. Therefore, Korean Christian theology in such an existential situation is compelled to deal with these different religious paradigms. As preparation for a Korean constructive theology, I have compared the confuciology of Wang Yang-ming (1472-1529) and the theology of Karl Barth (1886-1968). Similarities and Differences between Confucianism and Christianity appear most saliently in their understandings on the root-paradigm of humanity. In Wang's confuciology, the root paradigm of humanity is articulated as *liang-chih* (the innate knowledge of the good), the foundation of genuine humanity (*jen*) and reciprocity (*shu*), immanent in the human mind-and-heart: In Barth's theology of sanctification, it is *humanitas Christi* (the humanity of Christ) who perfected the image of God (*imago Dei*) through the realization of agapeic love on the cross. This chapter will compare these two crucial doctrines to explore the possibility of constructing a new christological paradigm through the reinterpretation of Confucianism. This chapter consists of three sections. The first section attempts an interpretation of Wang's doctrine of *liang-chih*, and the second section a summary of Barth's doctrine of *humanitas Christi*. Comparing these two doctrines, the final section explores the possibility of a theology-in-encounter in the Korean context, where a real encounter of the two great traditions for humanity, Confucianism and Christianity, has taken place historically.

1. *Liang-chih:* Inner Sage

1) The Great Principle

With the doctrine of *hsing chi li* (the nature [*hsing*] is the principle [*li*]), Chu Hsi's method of cultivation focused on the attitude of reverence (*ching*)[1] and the rigorous engagement in the investigation of principles (*ko-wu*). This reduced the status of mind-and-heart (*hsin*) to something inferior to nature (*hsing*). However, with the doctrine of *hsin chi li* (the mind-and-heart is the principle), Wang asserted that mind-and-heart and nature are identical and "coextensive."[2] The *hsin* itself has an innate or original ability to discern the Heavenly Principle (*T'ien-li*) and know the good. Borrowing the term from Mencius, Wang defined this primordial faculty of *hsin* as *liang-chih*.[3] Then *liang-chih* became "the great principle" of Wang's whole Neo-Confucian thinking.[4] Wang said:

> My idea is that it is incorrect to interpret the investigation of the principles of the things to the utmost as we come into contact with them to mean . . . devoting oneself to external things and neglecting the internal. If an unenlightened student can really carefully examine the Principle of Nature in the mind in connection with things and events as they come, and extend his innate or original knowledge of the good [*liang-chih*], then though stupid he will surely become intelligent and though weak he will surely become strong. The great Foundation will be established and the universal Way [in human relations] will be in operation. (CSL: 103)[5]

Like *hsin*, *liang-chih* has both affective and cognitive dimensions. It is a primordial feeling "prereflective and spontaneous"⁶ like the natural feeling of "alarm and commiseration" when we see a child about to fall into a well.⁷ At the same time, it is "nothing other than the Principle of Nature [*T'ien-li*] where the natural clear consciousness reveals itself. Its original substance is merely true sincerity and commiseration." (CSL: 176) It is a "revelation" of the Heavenly Principle (*T'ien-li*) in human original consciousness.⁸ It is the foundation of all knowledge, and "the great basis of learning and the first principle of the teaching of the Sage" (CSL: 150). It is the inherent moral "standard" (or "the inner forum") to judge right and wrong, which is the "true secret" of the Confucian project of self-cultivation.⁹

> Your innate knowledge¹⁰ is your own standard. When you direct your thought your innate knowledge knows that it is right if it is right and wrong if it is wrong. You cannot keep anything from it. Just don't try to deceive it but sincerely and truly follow it in whatever you do. Then the good will be preserved and evil will be removed. What security and joy there is in this! This is true secret of the investigation of things and the real effort of the extension of knowledge. (CSL: 193)

Wang also compared *liang-chih* to the "spiritual seal" of the Buddha-mind which can assure the truth, like "a gold-testing stone," a mariners' "compass," or "a wonder medicine" of Taoist alchemy, "one touch of which will turn iron into gold" (CSL: 194). Therefore, Tu Wei-ming rendered *liang-chih* as "primordial awareness." The primordial awareness, as "an innermost state of human perception wherein knowledge and action form a unity" or the "'humanity of the heart,' creates values of human understanding as it encounters the world."¹¹

Liang-chih is acquired not by a deliberate learning of a coded ethical knowledge, but naturally through an experiential realization (CSL: 156). However, when it encounters the world, deliberate efforts are also required to refine and clarify its meaning in the concrete context (CSL: 226). Such efforts are in fact essential to acquire our sensitivity and increase its precision toward *liang-chih.* They entail a serious hermeneutical engagement in Confucianism.

Wang illustrated by using two intriguing examples of Shun and Wu (CSL: 109-110). Sage-Emperor Shun married the two daughters of Emperor Yao without his parents' consent, which violated the conventional Confucian norm of filial piety. Sage-King Wu of Chou launched a military expedition against the house of Shang before burying his own father, which was also against the conventional practice of filial piety. However, Mencius approved their deeds as legitimate because of their greater motives that surpassed ordinary social conventions. For Shun, installing proper descendants was more essential than trying to obtain impossible permission from his parents. For Wu, saving the people, who suffered under the tyranny of King Chou of Shang, was more immediate than his father's funeral. Wang argued that they could do these unusual deeds according to the direction of *liang-chih* (CSL: 110).

Wang constituted *liang-chih* as the hermeneutical principle for the Classics. Wang's mature thought was *liang-chih*-centered. The Classics are merely "histories of *liang-chih* in action."[12] They are valuable only as paradigmatic records of the work of *liang-chih* in historical contexts (CSL: 23). Wang endorsed Lu Hsiang-shan's statement: "If in learning I understand what is fundamental, all the Six Classics are my footnotes."[13] Furthermore, sages are worthy as living paradigms of *liang-chih* in action. They illustrate the trajectory of *liang-chih* as "passing shadows." Wang said, "The thousand sages are all passing shadows; *Liang chih* alone is my teacher."[14]

Wang warned against literal interpretations of the Classics and of the deeds of the sages. The Classics and the sages were history, "and no more" (CSL: 23). Although they can show examples of *liang-chih* in action, they are not ends of self-cultivation, but only *liang-chih* is the goal. *Liang-chih*, as the hermeneutical principle, surpasses even the authority of Confucius (CSL: 159).

Wang created a "hermeneutical circle," holding *liang-chih* as the foreconception (*Vorgriff*) of his interpretative structure.[15] Wang appeared to engage in a project of demythologization, like that of Rudolf Bultmann. Demythologizing the values of the Classics and the sages, Wang emphasized the existential application of *liang-chih* here and now.[16] Wang wrote a poem.

> Each and every human mind has Confucius within,
> But afflicted by hearing and seeing,
> they become confused and deluded;
> Now I point to your true original face,
> It is none other than *liang-chih*—have no more doubts.[17]

Liang-chih is the inner sage or "sagehood," naturally endowed in all people.[18] Every person has *liang-chih*, whether a sage, worthy, or stupid. The difference among sage, worthy and ordinary people is not in quality but in quantity like that among "the sun in the clear sky," "the sun in the sky with floating clouds," and " the sun on a dark, dismal day" (CSL: 228). Since even a sage cannot extend *liang-chih* perfectly, everybody is ultimately the same. Every person has an innate power to strive to be an authentic human (there is the sun even in the dark sky). Wang's notion of *liang-chih* shows a strong egalitarianism. He discussed with his student.

> The Teacher said, "There is the sage in everyone. Only one has not enough self-confidence and buries his own chance." Thereupon he looked at Yü-chung and said, "From the beginning there is the sage in you." Yü-chung rose and said that he did not deserve it.
> The Teacher said, "This potentiality originally belongs to you. Why decline?"
> Yü-chung said again, "I do not deserve it."
> The Teacher said, "Everyone has this potentiality. How much more is that true of you, Yü-chung! Why be so modest? It won't do even if you are modest." (CSL: 194)

2) Self-Transcendence

The Doctrine of the Mean states:

> While there are no stirrings of pleasure, anger, sorrow, or joy, the mind may be said to be in the state of EQUILIBRIUM. When those feelings have been stirred, and they act in their due degree, there ensues what may be called the state of HARMONY. This EQUILIBRIUM is the great root *from which grow all the human actings* in the world, and this HARMONY is the universal path *which they all should pursue.* [19]

Accordingly, Ch'eng Yi defined *hsing* (nature) as the state of equilibrium (*chung*) before the rise of feelings, but *hsin* (the mind-and-heart) as the state after the feeling are aroused.[20] Chu Hsi also followed this distinction.[21] But Wang rejected this differentiation between nature and mind-and-heart, and rather identified *hsin*-in-itself (*hsin-chih-pen-t'I*), literally the original substance of the mind-and-heart) with *liang-chih*: "The equilibrium before the feelings are aroused is innate knowledge" (CSL: 136). The *hsin*-in-itself is a primordial, ontological state, in which any existential, ontic distinction of before and after, equilibrium and harmony, inner and external, or activity and tranquility becomes obsolete. It is a being-in-itself, analogous to Heidegger's notion of *Dasein*.[22]

> As the mind is neither before nor after any state, is neither internal nor external, but is one substance without differentiation. . . The state before the feelings are aroused exists in the state in which feelings have been aroused. But in this state there is not a separate state which is before the feelings are aroused. The state after the feelings are aroused exists in the state before the feelings are aroused. But in this state there is not a separate state in which the feelings have been aroused. Both are not without activity or tranquility and cannot be separately characterized as active or tranquil. (CSL: 137)

Liang-chih as the *hsin*-in-itself is a dynamic Being-in-itself, which penetrates and transcends such distinctions: "but innate knowledge makes no distinction between doing something and doing nothing" (CSL: 136). It is bright and transparent like the "shining mind" (CSL: 139f.) and the "bright mirror" (CSL: 148f.). Wang identified *liang-chih* with the Heavenly Principle (*T'ien-li*). Wang said, "Innate knowledge is where the Principle of Nature is clear and intelligent. Therefore innate knowledge is identical with the Principle of Nature." (CSL: 152) Furthermore, Wang identified *liang-chih*-in-itself (*liang-chih pen-t'i*, the original substance of *liang-chih*) with the Great Vacuity (*T'ai-hsü*),[23] the Neo-Confucian expression of the Ultimate Primordiality. Like the Great Vacuity, *liang-chih*-in-itself is absolutely self-transcendent:

> The vacuity of innate knowledge is the Great Vacuity of nature. The non-being of innate knowledge is the formlessness of the Great Vacuity. Sun, moon, wind, thunder, mountains, rivers, people, and things, and all things that have figure, form, or color, all function and operate within this formlessness of the Great Vacuity. None of them has become an obstacle to nature. The sage merely follows the functioning of his innate knowledge and Heaven, Earth, and all things are contained in its functioning and operation. How can there be anything to transcend innate knowledge and become its obstacle? (CSL: 220)

Furthermore, *liang-chih* as self-transcendence is the creative Spirit. It is "the spirit which creates all things, Heaven, Earth, ghosts, and gods. 'It is that to which there is no opposite [or equal].'"[24] *Liang-chih* as the creative Spirit capacitates cosmic differentiations through permeating all things and warrants them into the anthropocosmic identification. *Liang-chih* substantiates the unity among diversities and the cosmic interpenetration through the work of its *ch'i* (material force):

> The Innate knowledge of man is the same as that of plants and trees, tiles and stones. Without the innate knowledge inherent in man, there cannot be plants and trees, tiles and stones. This is not true of them only. Even Heaven and Earth cannot exist without the innate knowledge that is inherent in man. For at bottom Heaven, Earth, the myriad things, and man form one body. The point at which this unity is manifested in its most refined and excellent form is the clear

intelligence of the human mind. Wind, rain, dew, thunder, sun and moon, stars, animals and plants, mountains and rivers, earth and stones are essentially of one body with man. It is for this reason that such things as the grains and animals can nourish man and that such things as medicine and mineral can heal disease. Since they share the same material force [*ch'i*], they enter into one another. (CSL: 221f.)

3) Subjectivity: Radical Humanity

Liang-chih as *hsin*-in-itself is the life-giving true self:

Basically the original substance of the mind is none other than the Principle of Nature, and is never out of accord with propriety [*li*]. This is your true self. This true self is the master of the body. If there is no true self, there will be no body. Truly, with the true self, one lives; without it, one dies. (CSL: 80f.)

Tu Wei-ming enunciated *liang-chih* as "subjectivity," which means the true self or genuine humanity.[25] However, subjectivity is distinguished from subjectivism (egocentricism) or solipsism.[26] *Liang-chih* as subjectivity designates "the innermost and indissoluble reality" of humanity, never to be completely lost.[27] Hence, *liang-chih* signifies "radical humanity," in which radical means "of or from the root" (*radix*) or "going to the foundation."[28]

Liang-chih as subjectivity has both internality and universality. *Liang-chih* as internality has two meanings: the "clear illumination" (*chao-ming*) and "spiritual awareness" (*ling-chüeh*) of the Heavenly Principle. The clear illumination means "the penetrative insight that grasps the ultimate reality by a self-generative 'intellectual intuition.'"[29] And the spiritual awareness signifies "an all-embracing sensibility that embodies the whole universe by a self-sufficient 'anthropocosmic feeling.'"[30] However, *liang-chih*, as the intellectual intuition and the anthropocosmic feeling, must be extended beyond anthropocentric subjectivism. *Liang-chih* as universality is dynamic and self-transcendent, hardly localizable, but universally inter-penetrating. Hence, the great person who possesses radical humanity is defined not merely by the internal possession of *liang-chih* but also by its realization in the universal extension. In this respect, Wang articulated the doctrine of *Wan-wu yi-t'i* (literally, the Oneness of All Things):

> The great man regards Heaven, earth, and the myriad things as one body. He regards the world as one family and the country as one person. As to those who make a cleavage between objects and distinguish between the self and others, they are small men. That the great man can regard Heaven, Earth, and the myriad things as one body is not because he deliberately wants to do so, but because it is natural humane nature of his mind that he does so.[31]

The great person who possess radical humanity has "spiritual sensibility and loving care" of the cosmos as a whole.[32] This cosmic spiritual communion is possible because radical humanity is ontologically in an organismic unity with Heaven, Earth, and the myriad things. This vision of the "cosmic togetherness"[33] is well expressed in Chang Tsai's *Western Inscription*:

> Heaven is my father and Earth is my mother,
> and even such a small creature as I finds an intimate
> place in their midst.
> Therefore that which fills the universe I regard as my body
> and that which directs the universe I consider as my nature.
> All people are my brothers and sisters, and all things are
> my companions . . . .[34]

4) *Jen* (Humanity), the Paradigm of Humanity[35]

The Chinese character, *jen*, a cardinal Confucian virtue, is composed of a graph that means human being and two strokes that mean two. Etymologically, the word means two human beings, or togetherness of human beings. Thus, Peter A. Boodberg translated it as "co-humanity," "co-human," or "co-humanize."[36] As we saw in the passages already quoted, Wang not only expanded this togetherness dimension of *jen* to the cosmic level as Chang Tsai's *Western Inscription* had, but also developed further an ontology such as the doctrine of the Oneness of All Things.

> Forming one body with Heaven, Earth, and the myriad things is not only true of the great man. Even the mind of the small man is no different. Only he himself makes it small. Therefore, when he sees a child about to fall into a well, he cannot help a feeling of alarm and commiseration. This shows that his humanity [*jen*] forms one body with the child. It may be objected that the child belongs to the same species. Again, when he observes the pitiful cries and frightened appearance of birds and animals about to be slaughtered, he cannot help feeling an inability to bear their suffering. This shows that his humanity forms one body with birds and animals. It may be objected that birds and animals are sentient beings as he is. But when he sees plants broken and destroyed, he cannot help a feeling of pity. This shows that his humanity forms one body with plants. It may be said that plants are living things as he is. Yet, even when he sees tiles and stones shattered and crushed, he cannot help a feeling of regret. This shows that his humanity forms one body with tiles and stones. This means that the mind of the small man necessarily has the humanity that forms one body with all. Such a mind is rooted in his Heaven-endowed nature, and is naturally intelligent, clear, and not beclouded.[37]

Jen (humanity) as the paradigm of radical humanity (*liang-chih*) implies not only a manifested structure of radical human subjectivity but also a spiritual medium through which reconciliatory communions are made possible. Thus, *jen* is both cosmic togetherness—"The man of humanity regards all things as one body" (CSL: 226) -- and the life-giving spirituality—the "unceasing principle of production and reproduction" (CSL: 56).[38] For this reason, *jen* is also predicated as the "clear character" (*ming-te*), the first root metaphor of *The Great Learning*. However, in terms of the substance-function relationship, this predication defines its substance (the ontological structure). It requires that we put its functional counterpart (the ethico-religious realization), i.e., "loving the people" (*ch'in-min*),[39] the second root metaphor of *The Great Learning*, to universal extension:

> To manifest the clear character is to bring about the *substance* of the state of forming one body with Heaven, Earth, and the myriad things, whereas loving the people is to put into universal operation the *function* of the state of forming one body. Hence manifesting the clear character consists in loving the people, and loving the people is the way to manifest the clear character. Therefore, only when I love my father, the fathers of others, and the fathers of all men can my humanity really form one body with my father, the fathers of others, and the father of all men. When it truly forms one body with them, then clear character of filial piety will be manifested. . . . Everything from ruler, minister, husband, wife, and friends to mountains, rivers, spiritual beings, birds, animals, and plants should be truly loved in order to realize my humanity that forms one body with them, and then my clear character will be completely manifested, and I will really form one body with Heaven, Earth, and the myriad things. This is what is meant by manifesting the clear character throughout the world. This is what is meant by regulation of the family, ordering the state, and bringing peace to the world. This is what is meant by full development of one's nature.[40]

Wang's notion of loving the people has dynamic sociopolitical implications, by dynamically recovering the original structure of radical humanity. However, this love is prereflective and spontaneous like the feeling of commiseration. Its extension must follow the order of this natural feeling in social relations, e.g., the family, the society at large, and the world, and the universe (concrete-universal approach). But he argued against an ideal concept, like the Mohist's universal love, because it has a weak starting point and is vulnerable to the abuse of "leveling" natural affections and responsibilities.[41] Wang interpreted the notion of "relative importance" in *The Great Learning* to signify a built-in structure of order in the paradigm of radical humanity. According to this structure, he redefined four other cardinal Confucian virtues: righteousness (*i*), propriety (*li*), wisdom (*chih*), and faithfulness (*hsin*):

> What *The Great Learning* calls relative importance means that according to innate knowledge there is a natural order which should not be skipped over. This is called righteousness. To follow this order is called propriety. To understand this order is called wisdom. And to follow this order from beginning to end is called faithfulness. (CSL: 223)

In Wang's Confucian anthropology, human beings,[42] as bearers of *liang-chih*, are the mind-and-heart [*hsin*] of the universe (CSL: 166), or "the psychic center of the universe."[43] Etymologically human being, *homo*, (*jen*) is the same word as the common Chinese vocable *jen* (humanity).[44] Human beings in themselves are self-transcendent with innate spiritual powers for self-realization and have dynamic capacities for self-transformation. Human beings, alone in the cosmos, are capable of creative hermeneutics; they name things, understand, interpret, and make existential decisions. They permeate the whole universe through the dynamic force of their *ch'i*. They act as 'servants' of the sovereign *liang-chih*.[45] Their luminous spirits (*ling-ming*) are at the same time the masters of the universe. In short, human beings are the cosmic hermeneutical principle. Wang said:

> My luminous spirit is the master of Heaven-and-Earth and all things. If Heaven is deprived of my luminous spirit, who is going to look into its height? If Earth is deprived of my luminous spirit, who is going to look into its depth? If spiritual beings are deprived of my luminous spirit, who is going to distinguish between their good and evil fortune, or the calamities and blessings they will bring? Separated from my luminous spirit, there will be no Heaven, Earth, spiritual beings, or myriad things, and separated from these, there will not be my luminous spirit. They are all permeated with one material force [*ch'i*]. How can they be separated?[46]

2. *Humanitas Christi:* the Humanity of Christ

1) *Humanitas Christi*

In the *Church Dogmatics IV/2*,[47] Karl Barth formulated the doctrine of sanctification from Christology. Jesus Christ is both *vere Deus* (true divinity) and *vere homo* (true humanity), the formula used by traditional theology to fight against the docetic Gnosticism and Arianism. *Vere homo* involves God's complete assumption into humanity, making "a man as distinct from God, angel or animal, his specific creatureliness, his *humanitas*" (IV/2: 25). Different from a naturalist, idealist, or existentialist anthropology, Christian anthropology is first and foremost based on the *humanitas Christ* ("the humanity of Jesus Christ" [IV/2: 26]). Thus, Christology offers the basis for understanding anthropology. "A genuine knowledge of man in general, a theological anthropology, and therefore a theological doctrine of the sin and misery of man, can be based only on the particular knowledge of the man Jesus Christ, therefore on Christology" (IV/2: 27).

Humanitas Christi signifies not "an angel, a middle being, a demi-god," but "totally and unreservedly" human like us (IV/2: 27). The exaltation of Jesus in the New Testament means neither "a destruction or alteration of His humanity" nor an absolution of "His likeness with us, emptying it of its substance" (IV/2: 28), but "the exaltation of our essence with all its possibilities and limits into the completely different sphere of that totality, freedom, correspondence and service" (IV/2: 30). The humanity of Jesus Christ, "the basis and power of the atonement" (IV/2: 28) involves this upward movement in which the servant becomes the lord.[48] *Humanitas Christi* consists in three doctrines: (1) the gracious election of God, (2) the event of the incarnation, and (3) the resurrection and ascension of Christ (IV/2: 31).

(1) Election. *Humanitas Christi* "was and is and will be the primary content of God's eternal election of grace." For

"God's eternal grace is concretely the election of Jesus Christ." Hence, the humanity of Christ is "not merely *a* but *the* purpose of the will of God" (ibid.), "the primary object and content of the primal and basic will of God" (IV/2: 33).

(2) **Incarnation**. According to God's eternal election of grace, true humanity was historically fulfilled and actualized through the incarnation of God in the *humanitas Christi*. The incarnation is the ontic and noetic foundation of the Christology, "the *ratio essendi* and *ratio cognoscendi*, the ground of being and ground of knowledge" (IV/2: 37). In the event of incarnation, "without ceasing to be God" (IV/2: 40), Jesus Christ "becomes and is *also* true man" (IV/2: 41). Incarnation is one mode of "the work of the whole Holy Trinity" (IV/2: 44), *opera Trinitatis ad extra sunt indivisa* (the external works of the Trinity are undivided), being as the Son.[49] As a moment of the "intra-trinitarian life of God," *assumptio carnis* (the assumption of the flesh) takes places radically and totally and has opened a new "frontier" for humanity.[50] Incarnation involves four doctrinal aspects: (a) Jesus' becoming human; (b) His existence as human existence; (c) the unity of divine and human essence in Him; and (d) the exaltation of human essence to divine essence through Him.

(a) The incarnation, that "The Word became flesh," signifies "the becoming and being of God the Son in human essence" (IV/2: 46). It is an event, a God's own act, "a being which does not cease as such to be a becoming" (IV/2: 46). The efficacy of this *assumptio carnis* is inclusive, related not merely to "one man, but [also to] the *humanum* of all men, which is posited and exalted as such to unity with God" (IV/2: 49).

(b) The incarnation implies that the existence of the Son of God is that of a human being, a fellow person of the human race. "God Himself acts and suffers when this man acts and suffers as a human being . . . just because God Himself is its human subject in His Son." Barth endorsed the traditional doctrine of the hypostatic union, i.e., "the union made by God in the *hypostasis* (the mode of existence) of the Son" that is "the basis and power of the *nativitas Jesu Christi*," i.e., the conception and birth of Jesus through Mary (IV/2: 51).

(c) The incarnation indicates, "in the One Jesus Christ divine and human essence were and are united" (IV/2: 60). This unity must not be understood *"in abstracto*, not in a vacuum, not as the assertion of general truth;" but *"in concreto*, in the encounter with this one Subject, in the acknowledgment and recognition and confession of its particular truth" (IV/2: 61). The hypostatic union must not be conceived as an *a priori* possibility but as an *a posteriori* actuality.[51] The union of the two natures in Christ is "not itself a unity, but two-sided participation, the *communio naturarum*" (IV/2: 63). In this participation, Barth affirmed the Chalcedonian definition of Christological union, i.e., without confusion, change, division, and separation (see IV/2: 63-65).

(d) The incarnation signifies our exaltation; "as the Son of God became and is human, as He caused His existence to become that of a human being, as He united divine and human essence in Himself, He exalted human essence into Himself" (IV/2: 69). The mutual participation of divine and human essence in and by Jesus Christ involves the "twofold differentiation" (IV/2: 70) in both downward and upward directions. This mutual participation has a threefold meaning of impartation. The communication of attributes (*communicatio idiomatum*) relates to the impartation of the human essence to the divine and the divine to human in Jesus Christ. The communication of grace (*communicatio gratiarum*) refers to the fact that the human essence in Jesus Christ is totally determined by grace. And the communication of operations (*communicatio operatum*) pertains to "the common actualization of divine and human essence" (the union as act, not state) in Jesus Christ (IV/2: 104). This operation is "not just a divine *novum*, nor just a human"; On the contrary, "at one and the same time it is the great divine and the great human *novum*" (IV/2: 115).

(3) Resurrection and Ascension. This *novum* (newness) which is both divine and human actualizes and establishes "the knowing human subject" (IV/2: 120) in which the Holy Spirit is "the *doctor veritatis* [the teacher of the Truth]."[52] The resurrection and ascension of Jesus Christ are revelatory events of His self-declaration. Together, they are one "coherent" *event* (IV/2: 142) that has "a concrete element in human history at large," consists in "a series of concrete encounters and short conversations between the risen Jesus and His disciples" (IV/2: 143), and is "the concretely historical event of the self-manifestation of Jesus Christ after His death" (IV/2: 146). The resurrection and the ascension are "two distinct but inseparable moments in one and the same event" (IV/2: 150). If the resurrection refers to the *terminus a quo* (the point from which), the ascension means the *terminus ad quem* (the point o which). "The resurrection of Jesus Christ is the point of departure, the commencement of this history of revelation," signifying that Jesus came from the dead and rose again (IV/2: 151). "His ascension is the terminating point of this history of revelation," revealing that Jesus went to heaven (IV/2: 153): "He goes to the place of origin of all the dominion of divine power and grace and love. It is not only God who is now there, but as God is there He, this human being, is also there." (IV/2: 154) In this way, Jesus has opened an ontological space for humanity in heaven, which is the good news.

2) Royal Humanity

Barth enunciated four aspects of Jesus Christ as royal man (traditionally Christ's kingly office [*manus regium*]); (1) the distinctive presence of royal humanity, (2) royal humanity's likeness to God, (3) the accomplished life-act of royal humanity, and (4) the significance of cross for royal humanity.

(1) The presence of the royal man Jesus was distinctive and irrevocable. Jesus was present as a human being in encounter with others (IV/2: 156). In this encounter, Jesus demanded decision (IV/2: 157). His presence, as the presence of the Kingdom of God, was unforgettably distinctive (IV/2: 159). And He was "present irrevocably—in a way in which His existence was not compromised or broken by His death," both as the Son of Man and as the Son of God (IV/2: 163).

(2) The royal man in one mode of God's being exists as an eschatological revolutionary, heralding the Kingdom of God (IV/2: 126). Sharing "the strange destiny which falls on God in His people and the world" (IV/2: 167), the royal man "ignored all those who are high and mighty and wealthy in the world in favor of the weak and meek and lowly" (IV/2: 168). Barth would have agreed with the idiom of liberation theology "the preferential option for the poor."[53] He says, "In fellowship and conformity with this God who is poor in the world the royal man Jesus is also poor, and fulfills this transvaluation of all values, acknowledging those who are in different ways poor people as this world counts poverty" (IV/2: 169). The royal man's attitude to the established orders is genuinely revolutionary.[54] Setting "all programmes and principles in question" (IV/2: 172), the royal man deals with the world in His royal freedom,

> not in principle, not in the execution of a programme, but for this reason in a way which is all the more revolutionary, as the One who breaks all bonds asunder, in new historical developments and situations each of which is for those who can see and hear—only a sign, but an unmistakable sign, of His freedom and kingdom and over-ruling of history (IV/2: 173).

The "passive conservatism" (ibid.) that the royal man showed was "provisional." He did not ignore the temple, the order of family, the law, or provoke any direct conflict with economic and political relationships. However, "there is also no trace of any consistent recognition [of the relationships] in principle" (IV/2: 175). In fact, He assaulted radically and comprehensively not only the order of family and the prevailing religious order, but also the industrial, commercial, economic, and political *status quo*. He advocated a new bottle for a new wine, i.e., the invading kingdom of God: "the radical and indissoluble antithesis of the kingdom of God to all human kingdoms, the unanswerable question, the irremediable unsettlement introduced by the kingdom of God into all human kingdoms" (IV/2: 177). As the new cloth destroys the old garment, Jesus has actualized and fulfilled the new thing, completely ignoring and transcending the old order. Nevertheless, the royal man is "not against men but for men— even for men in all the impossibility of their perversion" (IV/2: 180). The decisive point is:

> [T]he royal man Jesus is the image and reflection of the divine Yes to man and his cosmos. It is God's critical Yes, dividing and disclosing and punishing with all the power of the sword. . . . But, like the Yes of God, it is really a Yes not a No, even though it includes and is accompanied by a powerful No. (IV/2: 180)

Hence, the New Testament beatitudes do not speak of "an empty paradox," but the declaration of Jesus the royal man— Lord of all humanity. They proclaim that earthly suffering, suffering actions, and voluntary suffering for His sake are not in vain. The beatitudes are "not merely a promise and proclamation, but the present impartation of full salvation, total life and perfect joy" (IV/2: 192).

(3) The life-act of the royal man Jesus is the root-paradigm of being human in the unity of being and acting: "His life *was* His act, and it has therefore the character of history" (IV/2: 193). Classical Christology divides the person and the work of Christ. However, in the life-act of royal humanity, the person and the work of Christ are not dualistic but identical. Moreover, His life-act shows the history of a Word in unity with deed, as the proto-paradigm of "human being as the doer

of the Word" (CD I/2, 18.1). The life-act of the royal man Jesus also manifests the unity of knowing and acting *par excellence* (cf. Wang).

> If we are to think of the speaking of Jesus as understood in the Gospel tradition, we must abandon completely the current distinctions between *logos* and *ethos*, or speaking and action, behind which there usually lurk the differentiations of knowledge and life, theory and practice, truth and reality (IV/2: 194).

The Word in the life-act of Jesus is not only the powerfully evangelizing, teaching, and heralding Word, but also a concretely, comprehensively, and a wholly *human* word (IV/2: 194-209). His concrete speech "always" accompanies His concrete activity. In His life-act, words and actions are in unity; "as His life-act was wholly His Word it was also wholly His activity, . . . His activity was as it were the kindling light of His speech—the light of the truth of His speech kindling into actuality" (IV/2: 209). His speaking constitutes an activity in a word, but neither remains to be "only" a word or an event in the spiritual sphere. The concrete speech accomplishes the corresponding concrete changes in the material and physical sphere of the world. "Not merely in part, but totally, His Word makes cosmic history" (IV/2: 209f.).[55]

> As a Word, therefore, it is also an action—an individual, concrete action as an individual, concrete indication of the fact that as a Word it is spoken in power. As an action it points to the fact that it is a Word which is spoken in fulfilled time by the One who fulfills it, so that it is no longer a promise, but itself that which is promised; a definite Word in the unequivocal form of a definite action. (IV/2: 210)

The acts of Jesus have an extraordinary, miraculous nature such as exorcism and healing. The miracles of Jesus (IV/2: 216-218) are "absolutely new and different' from all other usual, unusual, or supernatural occurrences (IV/2: 215). But they are mighty actualizations of "God's conclusive action, the coming of the new aeon" (IV/2: 219). The miracles imply God's radical blessing, election of humankind as His covenant-partner, and solidarity with humankind, and manifest the freedom of grace as the basis for human liberation.

In this context, faith is the necessary and corresponding "anthropological counterpart" to the free grace of God (IV/2: 243). Faith leads us to comprehend the miracles as signs of the coming kingdom and Jesus as the cosmic savior. Faith becomes the true basis of human freedom to communicate with God. In faith, those who attain the freedom of being God's partner become beings of unconditional and unlimited capacity. But Christian faith is not always identical with the general Christian concept of *credo*. Christian faith is specific, because the Christian encounter with Jesus Christ is "not like the sunrise illuminating a wide landscape from above, but like a single ray of light focused on one point and piercing what is otherwise an abyss of darkness." The metaphor of a single ray for Grace clearly describes the concrete-universal approach latent in Barth's theology. Christian faith works in a concrete-universal way, starting with the particular for the sake of the universal, corresponding to the freedom of grace that works like a single ray of light (in high density, specificity, and concentration). Grace has the total freedom to accomplish specific, and thus real, deliverance here and now; yet it concerns the whole human race in a most universal way.

> It is not just applied to all men equally. It is applied specifically to these particular men. In this particularity it is not merely a divine promise and therefore divine truth for all men here and now. As a sign for all men, but a sign set up then and there, it is a promise which is divinely fulfilled and truth which is divinely actualised. (IV/2: 246)

(4) The cross is the sign that "controls and penetrates and determines this whole" existence of the royal man (IV/2: 249). The cross is not alien, but central to the royal life of Jesus "whose story is finally the story of His passion" (IV/2: 250).

Paradoxically, the crucifixion of Jesus on the cross as the "final negative" signifies the foundation of all "positivities." In other words, the final negativity of the cross is the most concrete point, which opens the new aeon of universal positivities. The most concrete point in the Christian faith is this dangerous memory of the Crucified God-man in this final negativity, His innocent sufferings and voluntary death. However, the memory of the cross reveals and introduces the other inseparable, dangerous memory—the resurrection of royal humanity—the most universal point in Christian faith.

> In His passion the name of the God active and revealed in Him is conclusively sanctified; His will is done on earth as it is done in heaven; His kingdom comes, in a form and with a power to which as a man He can only give a terrified but determined assent. . . . In the deepest darkness of Golgotha He enters supremely into the glory of the unity of the Son with the Father. In that abandonment by God He is the One who is directly loved by God. . . . And it is not a new and specific secret. It is the secret of the whole. Nor is it a closed secret. It is a secret which has been revealed in the resurrection of Jesus. (IV/2: 252)

The crucifixion of Jesus on the cross was not just "the frightful paradox of a radical contradiction and destruction of the Son of Man," but, in fact, "the radical affirmation," the "overwhelming" "victory of the new actuality over the old." The disciples realized that it was the "coronation" of Jesus as the royal man" (IV/2: 254). His cross was no longer the symbol of hopelessness, but had become the solid basis and sign of both the eternal and temporal hope. His passion, including His prediction, is not "an anti-climax, but the climax of their witness" (IV/2: 255). All the witnesses of the Synoptics, John's Gospel, Pauline theology, and the first century Christians (IV/2: 255-258) are congruent in understanding the cross as "a decisive redemptive turning point." The cross has four implications: (a) a deeper dimension of death is "a more precise form of a readiness and willingness" (IV/2: 258). (b) The cross is the "must" for Jesus Christ according to both His voluntary self-determination and the predetermined divine order (IV/2: 259). (c) This "free but divinely ordained" giving-up actualized the finale to Israel's history and God's "handing over" to the people outside Israel in which "the Messiah of Israel becomes the Saviour of the world" (IV/2: 260). (d) "The 'must' of His passion extends to them [disciples] too" (IV/2: 263). The cross of the royal man becomes the light, power, glory, liberation, and hope for His disciples. Correspondingly, disciples must carry their own individual crosses, suffer their own afflictions, and bear the definite limitation of death so as to go after Christ and follow 'in his steps;' that is the secondary theology of the cross.

3) *Imago Dei* (the Image of God)

In the *Church Dogmatics*, Volume III/2, *The Creature*,[56] Barth articulated the nature of human being (or the real human nature) as (1) "real" human being (Sec. 44), (2) "humanity" (Sec. 45), and (3) "whole person" (Sec. 46).

(1) Real Human Being (human-to-God). Here again, Barth took Jesus Christ, who is a human being *for* God and God *for* human being, as the basis for defining real human being. Hence, Christology determines the formal and material dimensions of real human being. Formally, real human being consists in the right relationship with God, because human being is *"from, to,* and *with* God."[57] Materially, real human being is defined in four levels. (A real human being is "a being with Jesus [which] rests upon the election of God . . . [and] consists in the hearing of the Word of God" (III/2: 142). (b) Being a human "is a history" in a dynamic movement, but not a condition or a finished state (III/2: 157). (c) Human being is "a being in gratitude" (III/2: 166). Only as beings in gratitude are we to be real human beings in our own action, "not only the object but the subject of history" (III/2: 168). In this status, we are not only the object of God's grace in which God is the subject, but also the subject who responds with our thanksgiving to God as object. In other words, "the intersubjectivity of the interaction of grace (*charis*) and thanksgiving (*eucharistia*)" constitutes the content of human being.[58] (d) Real human nature is a being engaged in active responsibility to God. Real human being is the "subject in pure spontaneity" to the grace of God as well as its "object in pure receptivity" (III/2: 174). Human being in responsibility before God entails four inner notes: the knowledge of God, the obedience to God, the invocation of God, and the freedom that God imparts to us. At this point, Barth's theological anthropology moves toward a more inclusive understanding of human nature beyond the Christian terminology.

(2) Humanity (human-to-human). Jesus, the root-paradigm for humanity, is a human being for other human beings. Barth argued that, in the light of *humanitas Christi*, "humanity [*Menschlichkeit*] is to be described unequivocally as fellow-humanity [*Mitmenschlichkeit*]." The life-act of Jesus manifests that "man is the cosmic being which exists absolutely for its fellows" (III/2: 208). The paradigm of humanity as *Mitmenschlichkeit* is nothing but a copy [*Nachbild*] of the intratrinitarian life of the Triune God.[59] Between the being of God and the being of human, "there is correspondence and similarity;" that is to say, "There is an *analogia relationis*" (III/2: 220). The inner-trinitarian co-existence, co-inherence, and reciprocity in the eternal I-Thou relationship repeat and reflect in humanity as co-humanity. This *analogia relationis* (the analogy of relation) has been completely fulfilled in the *humanitas Christi*, the root-paradigm of humanity.

Furthermore, the humanity of Jesus is the image of God, the *imago Dei* (III/2: 219). The *humanitas Christi* as the *imago Dei* indicates, attests, and reveals the paradigm of humanity as *Mitmenschlichkeit* in the *analogia relationis* to the inner being of God. Barth said,

> Man generally, the man with the fellow-man, has indeed a part in the divine likeness of the man Jesus, the man for the fellow-man. As man generally is modeled on the man Jesus and His being for others, and as the man Jesus is modeled on God, it has to be said of man generally that he is created in the image of God. He is in his humanity, therefore in his fellow-humanity. God created him in His own image and the fact that He did not create him alone but in this connexion and fellowship. For in God's action as the Lord of the covenant, and even further back in His action as the Creator of a reality distinct from Himself, it is proved that God Himself is not solitary, that although He is one in essence He is not alone, but that primarily and properly He is in connexion and fellowship. It is inevitable that we should recall the triune being of God at this point. God exists in relationship and fellowship. As the Father of the Son and the Son of the Father He is Himself I and Thou, confronting Himself and yet always one and the same in the Holy Spirit. God created man in His own image, in correspondence with His own being and essence. . . . Because He is not solitary in Himself, and therefore does not will to be so *ad extra*, it is not good for man to be alone, and God created him in His own image, as male and female. This is what is emphatically said by Gen. 1:27, and all other explanations of the *imago Dei* suffer from the fact that they do not do justice to this decisive statement. . . . God is in relationship, and so too is the man created by Him. This is his divine likeness. When we view it in this way, the dispute whether it is lost by sin finds a self-evident solution. It is not lost. But more important is the fact that what man is indestructibly as he is man with the fellow-man, he is in hope of being and action of the One who is his original in this relationship." (III/2: 323f.)

Barth identified the image of God as togetherness, the plurality of I-Thou relationship. In his *Table Talk*, Barth further said:

> Image in Genesis I means that like God, who is living but not isolated (*Elohim* denotes plurality), there is plurality in man. Man has plurality like God, who is plural. Being man means being in togetherness: man [Adam] and wife [Eve]. . . . 'Living God' means 'togetherness'. . . . Image has a double meaning: God lives in togetherness with Himself, then God lives in togetherness with man, then men live togetherness with one another.[60]

Since the basic form of humanity is determined as the "being with others," being human entails "a determination" of being with others (III/2: 243). The statement "I am" presupposes the condition "I am in encounter" (III/2: 247). Barth put this relationship into the formula, "I am as Thou art" (III/2: 248), meaning a dynamic and essential encounter between two histories of two beings of I and Thou. In short, humanity is determined as the historical actualization of the being-in-encounter, in which the statement "I am as Thou art" is being realized. Humanity as being-in-encounter means "two-sided openness" (III/2: 251), a reciprocal intercommunication, and "mutual assistance in the act of being" (III/2: 260) in the history of encounter between I and Thou. Barth used the analogy of a fish that needs water to argue for this awareness of sociality as the structure of humanity (III/2: 263). Humanity as being-in-encounter stands for joyful co-humanity (*Mitmenschlichkeit*).[61] This common joy realizes "the freedom of encounter" from the ontological freedom of being a human as a creature (III/2: 272).[62] Human nature or the nature of humanity involves "freedom in the co-existence of man and man in which the one may be, and will be, the companion, associate, comrade, fellow and helpmate of the other" (III/2: 276).[63]

(3) The Whole Person (human-to-self). The *humanitas Christi* is the paradigm and norm of the whole person in the unity and proper order of soul and body. The basis of human soul and body is the Spirit. The foundation of human being as soul and body is the action of God's Spirit as the Creator, the Preserver, and the Redeemer. In other words, the Spirit is its irresistible and irreversible context and background to being authentically (in Barth's term, naturally) human. In this context, human being as a spirit has a space to be a subject as a natural human being, but not merely as an absorbed substructure of the divine being. To protect this human subjectivity, Barth made a distinction between the Spirit as Redeemer and the Spirit as the Creator and the Sustainer. In the Spirit as the Creator and Sustainer, Barth underscored the primordial ties of human beings in general with God and with other human beings prior to redemption.

Human nature is constituted as an interconnected unity within which there is an antithesis; namely, between "creaturely life" and "creaturely being" (III/2: 367). The creaturely life which refers to the soul designates a *living* being, i.e., a person's temporal existence, whereas the creaturely being, the body, is a living *being*, i.e., one's spatial form. Barth rejected the dualistic understanding of body and soul, refuting both extreme spiritualization and extreme materialization. The soul, the inner movement in time, perceives, experiences, thinks, feels, and decides; however, its full enactment necessitates the body, the outer movement in space. The freedom of "natural" human being signifies self-determination. However, human being cannot function as subjectivity with this capacity and freedom, apart from its material body. The soul and the body can be distinguished, but cannot be separated. They are completely interconnected so that a denial of this interconnectedness means a distortion of human nature.

Human nature is both a percipient being and an active being. Perception consists of a compound act of awareness (outer) and thought (inner). Although the former is distinctively related to the body and the latter to the soul, perception is an inseparable, single act of the whole person. But awareness and thought are primarily the acts of the soul, and secondarily those of the body. Action also consists of a compound act of desire (outer) and will (inner). In a similar manner to perception, desire and will are an inseparable single action, though desire is distinctively bodily and will soulful. They are also primarily of the soul and secondarily of the body. By willing, we can choose, determine, and make up our mind as to our desire. Being a whole person requires a discipline to preserve the order of human nature as the soul of the body.

3. *Liang-chih* and *Humanitas Christi*: Sage Meets Christ

1) *Liang-chih* and *Humanitas Christi*

Liang-chih (the innate knowledge of the good) and *humanitas Christi* (the humanity of Christ) present the Confucian and Christian visions of full humanity, the root-paradigms of radical humanity. Whereas *humanitas Christi* is the incarnation of the Word (logos) in history, *liang-chih* is the primordial awareness of immanent-transcendence in the human mind-and-heart. While both *liang-chih* and *humanitas Christ* are somewhat related to the notion of incarnation, though it is hidden in the Confucian case, their emphases are different. Wang thematized incarnate wisdom as the innate knowledge of good (or inner sage), whereas Barth understood the *assumptio carnis* of Jesus Christ as the Son of God. Wang focused on immanent potentiality, while Barth emphasized historical revelation.

Wang's doctrine of *liang-chih*: The genius of Wang is in his thematization of *liang-chih* as the transcendent subjectivity of humanity. *Liang-chih* is the great principle of Wang's mature Neo-Confucian thinking. He reasserted that mind-and-heart is identical and coextensive with original human nature (*hsin chi li*). Mind-and-heart, as a heavenly endowment, has an innate, or original, ability to discern the Heavenly principle and know the good. Wang defined this primordial faculty of mind-and-heart as *liang-chih*. Involving both cognitive and affective dimensions, *liang-chih* entails a prereflective knowledge and spontaneous natural feeling. As the innate knowledge of the Heavenly principle in human original consciousness, it is also called the 'primordial awareness'—'an innermost state of human perception' which generates values of human understanding as it encounters the world.

Wang's mature confuciology is *liang-chih*-centered. *Liang-chih* is taken as the hermeneutical principle for all the

Confucian *Classics*. Exemplary deeds of the Confucian sages are regarded as the 'histories of *liang-chih* in action.' Furthermore, Wang advocates a radically egalitarian perspective; *liang-chih*, the inner sage, is a natural endowment of all people. The distinction between sage and ordinary people is not in quality, but in quantity, the degree of extension. Every person has some innate power to exert the self to be authentically human.

In Neo-Confucian metaphysics, *liang-chih* is in a state of equilibrium before feelings are aroused. Wang identifies it with the mind-and-heart-in-itself, which is a Confucian notion of being-in-itself analogous to Heidegger's *Dasein*. *Liang-chih*, dynamic being-in-itself, transcends all dualistic distinctions and penetrates everything. Wang identifies *liang-chih*-in-itself with the Great Vacuity, the Neo-Confucian expression for the Ultimate Primordiality. Like the Great Vacuity, *liang-chih*-in-itself is self-transcendent. And this self-transcendent *liang-chih* is also the creative Spirit that enables cosmic differentiations and assures them into the anthropocosmic identification through the work of its material force (*ch'i*).

Furthermore, *liang-chih* is the life-giving True Self, the "subjectivity" of genuine humanity. *Liang-chih*, as the 'innermost and indissoluble reality' of humanity, is radical humanity that has both internality and universality. Internality means both "a self-generative intellectual intuition" and "a self-sufficient anthropocosmic feeling."[64] But these internal dimensions are to be extended beyond anthropocentric subjectivism in universal extension (*chih liang-chih*), where all things are in unity. Radical humanity in the Confucian anthropocosmic vision envisages "cosmic togetherness" in the triadic unity of Heaven, Earth, and the myriad things which entails 'a spiritual sensibility and loving care' with the cosmos as a whole.

Barth's doctrine of *humanitas Christi*: Barth's Christ-centered theology establishes the foundation of sanctification on *humanitas Christi*, the being and becoming of Jesus Christ in human existence (CD IV/2). The doctrine of *humanitas Christi* is related to election, incarnation, and resurrection and ascension. The humanity of Christ, both the electing God and the elected humanity, is the root-paradigm of God's gracious election. The incarnation (*assumptio carnis*) of Jesus' becoming and being of human existence, in totality, signifies ultimately the exaltation of human essence to divine essence. The resurrection and ascension are an inseparable, revelatory and historical event in which the risen Christ manifests Himself as the ultimate foundation of sanctification.

Hence, *humanitas Christi* involves the threefold concrete-universal act of God. First, *humanitas Christi* was the concrete-universal manifestation of God's election of the human race. Second, the *assumptio carnis* of the Triune God in the particular person Jesus (incarnation) was the historical, and thus the concrete, fulfillment of God's salvific love for the human race. Third, the event of resurrection and ascension of the particular humanity of Jesus has opened once and for all the ontological basis for the redemption of the humankind, and thus has established the universal foundation for the exaltation of the human race. Through the humanity of Christ in these events of election, incarnation, and resurrection and ascension, God has accomplished His gracious will to humanity as His covenant partner. Hence, the humanity of Christ is the revelation of God's most concrete-universal way of including humanity in His intratrinitarian history that establishes the ontological space of human sanctification. At the same time, *humanitas Christi* is God's presentation of the most concrete-universal paradigm of humanity.

Royal Man Christology: *Humanitas Christi* as the most concrete-universal humanity was manifested in the life-act of the royal man Jesus (traditionally, the kingly office). The royal man Jesus (as both the paradigm of full humanity and a mode of God's being) exhibits a revolutionary attitude "in a preferential option for the poor" against the exploitative established order. His life-act is the history of the Word in unity with deed (the unity of speech and act). Also it manifests the unity of knowing and acting, being and doing, hence theology and ethics. In other words, the life-act of the royal man Jesus reveals the paradigm of the unity of knowing and acting and theology and ethics *par excellence*. Paradoxically, the cross of Jesus, the final negativity, constitutes all-embracing positivities (the resurrection). The cross, the most concrete point of the Christian faith, opens the new aeon of universal actualities. This dangerous memory of the Crucified, the most concrete point of the Christian faith, points to the inseparable dangerous memory of the resurrection of the Crucified, the most universal point of the Christian faith.

Liang-chih and *humanitas Christi*:   *Liang-chih* and *humanitas Christi* are the centers and hermeneutical principles of Wang's confuciology and Barth's theology. *Liang-chih* and *humanitas Christi* are the foundations for self-cultivation and sanctification. Both of them articulate radical humanity—full, real, authentic, and true human subjectivity—the root paradigm for radical humanization. These two central notions of Wang and Barth provided their salient material points of convergence and divergence, constituting the bases for further discussions.

Some points of convergence: First, both Wang and Barth took these comparable root-paradigms as the hermeneutical principle for understanding their texts and traditions. Whereas Wang's confuciology is *liang-chih*-centered, Barth's theology is Christ-centered. Second, Humanitas *Christi* converges with *liang-chih*, because the former also works as "good knowing." The knowledge of Christ reveals the specificities of sin, just as *liang-chih* (the primordial awareness) illuminates evil. Third, they are congruent in their radical assertion of the inseparability of ontological knowledge and ethical practice. While *liang-*

chih manifests the proto-paradigm of the unity of knowing and acting, the life-act of Christ reveals the historical paradigm par excellence of the unity of logos and ethos, theory and praxis, and theology and ethics. Fourth, both manifest the most concrete-universal. We have seen *humanitas Christi* as the most concrete-universal of the Christian faith. We also could say that *liang-chih* is the most concrete-universal in the Wangian sense, the concrete-universal of humanity as well as of the Heavenly *Tao*. Fifth, both *liang-chih* and *humanitas Christi* as the most concrete-universal are self-transcendent, life-giving human subjectivity (true self).

Some points of divergence: First, these two concrete-universals have divergent conceptual contexts. Whereas *liang-chih* is based on the anthropocosmic vision of immanent-transcendence, *humanitas Christi* is founded on faith in the gracious election of God (salvation history).[65] Second, hence, their points of departure are divergent. While Wang begins by thematizing *liang-chih* with an immanent potentiality in the human mind-and-heart, Barth thematized it with the humanity of Christ in historicality and personal incarnation. Third, they have accordingly different foci. Whereas confuciology focuses on ontological identification (e.g., the unity of all things), theology concentrates relatively on existential differentiation (e.g., the problem of evil). Fourth, thus, there is a nuance in the characterization of their root-paradigms. Whereas *liang-chih* is viewed as inner sage (immanent-transcendence), Jesus Christ is an historical and personal incarnation (historico-transcendence). Fifth, this nuance constitutes their strengths and weakness. On the one hand, confuciology is strong in its all-embracing, anthropocosmic-sapiential articulation, and relatively weak in dealing with the historical-existential problems of the human predicament, suffering, and death. On the other hand, theology is strong in dealing with existential-historical problems, while falling easily into an exclusivism, fundamentalism, or historical anthropocentricism.

	Wang	**Barth**
Root-paradigm	*liang-chih*	*humanitas Christi*
Most concrete-universal	of immanent transcendence	of election/ incarnation
Subjectivity	radical humanity	royal humanity
Ethical paradigm	unity of knowing and acting	unity of theology and ethics
Good knowing	Good and evil	Christ and sin
Characterization	inner sage	historical incarnation
	immanent-transcendence	historico-transcendence
Focus	immanent potentiality	historicality
	ontological identification	existential differentiation

2) *Jen and Imago Dei (Mitmenschlichkeit)*

Heuristically, the root-paradigms, *liang-chih* and *humanitas Christi*, can be divided into two dimensions: vertical (transcendental) and horizontal (human-to-human). Although their articulations on the vertical dimension differ (immanent-transcendence and historico-transcendence), those on the horizontal dimension, the Confucian notion of *jen* and Barth's understanding of the image of God show a remarkable (substantial) point of convergence, the same conclusion that the ontological paradigm of humanity is creative or joyful co-humanity (*Mitmenschlichkeit*), being-with-others or being-in-togetherness.

The Confucian notion of *Jen*: Etymologically, *jen* (humanity), the cardinal Confucian virtue, means togetherness of human beings, "co-humanity," or "co-humanization." Confucians expand *jen*'s notion of togetherness to the cosmic dimension; namely, the cosmic togetherness represented in the organismic unity of Heaven, Earth, and the myriad things (Wang's doctrine of the unity of all things). *Jen* as cosmic togetherness entails a spiritual sensibility and loving care with the cosmos as a whole. *Jen*, a manifested structure of radical humanity, is a life-giving, creative spirituality through which reconciliatory communion is made possible. In terms of *The Great Learning*, *jen*, as the substance, is "the clear character" (the ontological structure of radical humanity), while *jen*, as function, is "the loving people" (the ethico-religious realization of radical humanity). This functional dimension of the loving people has a dynamic socio-political implication. However, such a concept as "universal love" is not tenable, from this vantage point, because it is abstract and vulnerable to misuse (cf. Barth's concept of *agape*). Rather, it must be manifested in a concrete-universal way.

Humanity (*jen*) in Chinese is etymologically the same word and has the same pronunciation as human being (*jen*). Human beings, as bearers of radical humanity, are the mind-and-heart of the universe. Human beings possess innate spiritual powers for self-realization and dynamic capacities for self-transformation. Human beings as sole servants of the sovereign *liang-chih* participate in the cosmic hermeneutical process of reconciliation, transformation, and nourishment.

Barth's understanding of *Imago Dei*: In the doctrine of creation (CD III/2), Barth formulated the paradigm of human as (1) real human being in relation to God (vertical), (2) humanity in relation to others (horizontal), and (3) the whole person in relation to self (selfhood). (1) Analogously to Jesus Christ who is from, to, and with God, real human being is defined as a person with Jesus in the hearing of the Word of God, as a historical being in gratitude, and as subjectivity in pure spontaneity to the grace of God. (2) Since Jesus is a human being with and for other human beings, a person is the cosmic being that exists absolutely with and for its fellow beings. In the paradigm of Jesus, humanity (*Menschlichkeit*) means a joyful co-humanity (*Mitmenschlichkeit*). This image of God, fulfilled in the *humanitas Christi*, signifies humanity as co-humanity, being-in-encounter, life-in-fellowship, or history-in-partnership. Analogous to intra-trinitarian co-existence, co-inherence, and reciprocity, humanity, as image of God, means a plurality as being-in-togetherness or a being-with-others. (3) Jesus Christ is also the paradigm of the whole person in the unity of soul and body. The human nature of the whole person is constituted by an interconnected unity of creaturely life (soul) and creaturely being (body).

Jen and Imago Dei: Barth's understanding of *imago Dei*—the paradigm of humanity as joyful *Mitmenschlichkeit*—is remarkably convergent with the Confucian perception of *jen* (humanity) as creative co-humanity. This entails an important, material point of convergence: Humanity (*jen* or *Menschlichkeit*) is co-humanity (*jen* or *Mitmenschlichkeit*).

Furthermore, Barth's third notion of the whole person, as integrated soul and body resonates strikingly with Wang's characterization of confuciology as "the learning of the body and mind" (*shen-hsin chih hsüeh*).[66] Self-cultivation emphasizes the integration of body and mind-and-heart (cf. *ch'eng-i*). The Chinese *shen*, the last character of the Chinese word for self-cultivation, originally denotes body but means a person in totality. Bracketing off the Christian vertical dimension (though we could also find a similar Confucian notion), both Wang and Barth hold the same understanding of being human: being human in both Confucian and Christian senses means being radically human, that is, a radical realization of being-in-togetherness in the unity of body and soul.

However, their divergent emphases—immanence and historicality—also appear in this case. Whereas Wang extended the notion of togetherness to the cosmic dimension (the unity of all things), Barth focused on the meaning of co-humanity within the historical dimension.

	Wang	**Barth**
Root Paradigm	*liang-chih*	*humanitas Christi*
Horizontal dimension	*jen*	*imago Dei*
Co-humanity	*jen* being-in-togetherness	*Mitmenschlichkeit* life-in-fellowship
Implication	cosmic togetherness	history-in-partnership

3) Wisdom Meets Christ: A New Paradigm of Anthropology

In this comparison between Wang's doctrine of *jen* and Barth's doctrine of *imago Dei,* we see two important implications: a material point of convergence and a complementary possibility between confuciology and theology. First of all, Wang's confuciology and Barth's theology completely met each other in the understanding of the horizontal dimension of humanity; that is to say, co-humanity, being-in-togetherness, life-in-fellowship, history-in-partnership, or inclusive being-in-encounter. This converging point reveals a proper place for the collision and fusion of the two great hermeneutical horizons, Confucianism and Christianity, and introduces a new horizon that a Christian theology of Confucianism can contribute to the Christianity and Confucianism in the coming civilization.

Secondly, we find a possibility that each doctrine complements the weaknesses of the other. On the one hand, the Christian historical consciousness would challenge confuciology to awaken from the state of "dreaming innocence" immersed under the naive anthropocosmic vision.[67] On the other hand, underscoring the ontological, organismic connection between humanity and nature, the Neo-Confucian understanding of human being as a cosmic being-in-togetherness would be a corrective to liberate theology from the captivity of an anthropocentric understanding of historical process, which, some say, is responsible for the present ecological crisis. This suggests a new paradigm of anthropology, inclusive humanity beyond both the violence of historical anthropocentricism and the naiveté of anthropocosmic vision.

Today, the issue of recovering humanity as cosmic togetherness has global significance. The future of the human race and the planet earth appear gloomy and apocalyptic, with merciless technological warfare, massive ecological disasters, the collapse of the balance of ideologies, grinding poverty killing millions of people, etc. The vicious circle of distrust, violence, and dehumanization continues to expand. This situation calls for radical humanization, once again, with its assuring trust and confidence in the original humanity, a creative, inclusive being-in-encounter in historico-cosmic togetherness.

4. The Tao of Jesus Christ

1) Jesus Christ as the Sincerity (*Ch'eng*) *Par Excellence*

In the encounter between Wang's doctrine of *liang-chih* and Barth's doctrine of *humanitas Christi*, we also find that Confucian insights are so illuminating that they can make profound contributions to the Christian understanding of Christ. For example, by using some Confucian concepts, we can reiterate Barth's doctrine of *humanitas Christi* even more transparently.

First, as we have seen, Barth's deliberations on *humanitas Christi* can be summarized in terms of the threefold concrete-universal act of God. Through the events of election, incarnation, and resurrection and ascension that consummate the divine-human transformation of turning the most concrete into the most universal, God accomplished His gracious will to humanity as His covenant partner once and for all. The *humanitas Christi* manifests both the most concrete-universal way through which God includes humanity within His intratrinitarian history and the most concrete-universal paradigm of humanity.

Second, the unity of word and deeds, which Barth emphasized in his Christology of royal man, can be articulated more clearly by the Confucian concept of *ch'eng* (sincerity). The Chinese character *ch'eng* made of two graphs that mean word (or speech) and accomplishment (or action) denotes sincere actualization of one's word. *Ch'eng* signifies the actualization of the unity of being and becoming through the unity of speaking and acting. With this concept of *ch'eng,* we can reiterate what Barth's Christology of royal man intends to elaborate through the life-act of Jesus. The life-act of Jesus Christ is the history of a Word in unity with deeds. In his life-act, there is no distinction between *logos* and *ethos*, or speaking and action. Hence, the life-act of Jesus can be articulated as the historical manifestation of the *ch'eng*-sincering par excellence.

Finally, we can sum up Barth's Christology as following: The sincere person Jesus, both in genuine humanity and one mode of God's being, has a revolutionary attitude to the established order with the preferential option for the poor. His life-act is the history of Word in unity with deed, that is to say the history of *ch'eng*-sincering. While the incarnation of the *humanitas Christi* refers to the concrete-universal embodiment of God's sincerity toward humanity in the anthropocosmic history, the life-act of Sage Jesus represents the paradigm of radical humanity in the unity of being and acting. The life-act of royal humanity manifests the paradigm of humanity *par excellence* in the unity of knowing and acting and of theology and ethics. Therefore, *humanitas Christi* reveals the most concrete-universal of the divine-human drama of reconciliation, and illustrates, as the ultimately sincere person, the root-paradigm of radical humanity in action. The miracles of Jesus Christ manifest the unity *par excellence* of human speech and cosmic transformation. The cross, as the most concrete signpost of the Christian faith, opens the new aeon of universal actualities. While the most concrete point of the Christian faith is the dangerous memory of the Crucified God-man in the final negativity, the dangerous memory of the resurrection of the Crucified, its inseparable end, is the most universal point of the Christian faith. On the cross, the royal man Jesus reveals the root-paradigm of radical humanity in utterly self-giving love (*agape*) and consummates the concrete-universal drama of the Triune God with the world.

2) The Tao of Jesus Christ: Toward a New Paradigm of Christology

From this vantage point, there were legitimate reasons in the *Ch'eng* christologies formulated by the first Korean theologian Yi Pyŏk and contextual theologian Yun Sung-bum.[68] Although much improved by Barth, today, royal Christology (kingly office) is anachronistic and no longer effective because it is the doctrine in the political paradigm of monarchism. It has many doctrinal problems in terms of political theology. Hence, rather than insisting the old royal Christology, it would be more proper, effective, and even accurate to conceive Christ as the ultimate humanity, Sage, who realized and revealed the humanity in complete sincerity.

Furthermore, the encounter of *liang-chih*, an expression of Confucian soteriology, and *humanitas Christi*, the foundation of Christian faith, illuminates a possibility for a more adequate Christology for Korean and other East Asian Christians. On the crucial question of Jesus, "Who do you say I am?" (Mt. 16:15), we East Asian Christians have followed the Western confessions of faith too easily and quickly, without the necessary process of critical and serious scrutinization. However, as we have seen, the Confucian paradigm has a great potential to make profound contributions to interpreting the traditional Christology. The traditional Western paradigms are no longer sufficient for us. We need a more appropriate paradigm to articulate our faith in Christ from our own depths. We need to go one step forward.

I am not suggesting a cheap religious syncretism. The reason for the long flourishing of the Western theology, no matter how you assess it, is because there was the paradigm of logos. The theological tradition had emerged as primitive Christianity accommodated the Greek philosophical concept, logos. Logos-centric theo-logies have dominated Western Christianity. The logos Christology embedded in the Nicene and Chalcedonian creeds developed as the Christian faith encountered Greek Philosophy, and has maintained the role to articulate the confessions for Western communities of faith. However, in this postmodern age, contemporary communities of faith have realized that such a logocentric or "phonocentric" theology has reached its limit and is almost bankrupt.[69] Now, global churches are searching for a new paradigm that enables them to make a more appropriate confession of faith. They are experiencing the birth pangs to produce a new paradigm for theology. May our new interpretation of the Tao of Christ based on our paradigm open new horizons to bring forth genuinely religious, holistic, practical, ecologically constructive, and cosmo-life centric theologies beyond the scientific, analytic, metaphysical, ecologically destructive, historico-anthropocentric theologies in decay?

First of all, the Tao (the Way) of Jesus Christ is a more preferable term than Christology. Jesus called himself the Way (John 14:6). Neither theo-logy, nor Christo-logy, but the Greek *hodos* (the Way, also meaning path, road, route, journey, march, etc.) was an original name of Christianity (see Act 9:2;

19:9; 22:4; 24:14, 22). Hence, Jürgen Moltmann was correct to use the title *The Way of Jesus Christ* in his book on Christology.[70] He said, the way-metaphor "embodies the aspect of process," makes us aware that every human christology is historically conditioned and limited," and involves "an invitation" to follow "christopraxis."[71] He further said, "I am trying to think of Christ no longer statically, as one person in two natures or as a historical personality. I am trying to grasp him dynamically, in the forward movement of God's history with the world."[72] In the Confucian paradigm, "one person in two natures of Christ" or "the person and work of Christ" would not be so much of a problem as an issue in the wrong direction. The Confucian insight of Tao may enable us to bring in important christological dimensions even more profoundly than Moltmann's term christopraxis can.

Second, we could conceive Jesus Christ as the Paradigm of Humanity (*Imago Dei* and *Jen*). Christ the Sage is a human being with and for other human beings. The humanity of Christ the Sage in the image of God illustrates the paradigm of humanity (*jen*) as co-humanity, being-in-togetherness, being-in-encounter, life and history-in-partnership. Traditional western theologies tend to remain under the captivity of anthropocentricism and historicism. Sage Christology may overcome this problem, introducing its environmental and cosmic dimensions (e.g., Christ as cosmic togetherness). The Confucian model of reciprocity and mutuality in anthropocosmic interaction would promote liberation of humanity and nature from the model of domination and exploitation.[73]

Finally, we could articulate Jesus Christ as the Ultimate Embodiment of *Liang-chih,* the Wisdom. Christ the Sage is the historical culmination of the immanent-transcendence in the human mind-and-heart. Jesus Christ, traditionally the incarnate *logos* can be thematized as the personal/historical embodiment of *liang-chih* in which human subjectivity has been completely identified with the ontological reality (*T'ien-li*). Christ as the ultimate historization of the anthropocosmic vision can be understood as the culmination of being human in action as the hermeneutical principle of cosmic communion. Then, in Christ the *Liang-chih*, the two concrete-universal stories of humanity and of God on humanization are fully encountered. Thus, these stories go beyond dialogue and are transformed into the story of inclusive human being, new human subjectivity, the novel paradigm of radical humanity in the cosmic anthropo-theistic theater and in the new aeon.

Since the primitive Christian church encountered Greek philosophy, Christianity has continued to blossom as a theology-in-encounter, namely, the logos theology. However, now the logos theology is waning. The coming world calls for a new theology-in-encounter. Furthermore, in the light of Wang Yang-ming and Karl Barth, human being in itself is a being-in-encounter, and radical humanization is the historical actualization of togetherness-in-encounter. Hence, the theology of genuine humanity needed for the communities of faith in the coming civilization is after all a creative and inclusive theology-in-encounter, as the Triune God is the creative and inclusive Being-in-encounter. And an essential Confucian and Christian contribution to the coming civilization can be made from the common assertion that humanity is the creative and inclusive being-in-encounter.

Notes

[1] *Ching* is an important notion of the Ch'eng-Chu school that is also translated as "seriousness" or "mindfulness." See Chan Wing-tsit, trans. and ed., *Neo-Confucian Terms Explained* (The Pei-hsi tzu-i) *by Ch'en Ch'un, 1159-1223)*, 100ff.; and Michael C. trans. and ed., *To Become a Sage: the Ten Diagrams on Sage Learning by Yi T'oegye* (New York: Columbia University Press, 1988), 212ff.

² Ching, *To Acquire Wisdom: The Way of Wang Yang-ming* (New York: Columbia University Press, 1976), 107.

³ This term is difficult to translate, as appeared in the following translations: "good conscience" (*liang-hsin*), "innate knowledge" (Wing-tsit Chan), "conscious wisdom" (Thomé H. Fang), "intuitive knowledge of the good" (David S. Nivison), "conscientious consciousness" (T'ang Chün-i), "subjectivity" or "primordial awareness" (Tu Wei-ming), "knowledge of the good" (Julia Ching), or "pure knowing" (Philip Ivanhoe). The term in the Chinese romanization will be used unless translation is necessary.

⁴ Ching, *Wisdom*, 107.

⁵ Chan Wing-tsit, trans., *Instructions for Practical Living and Other Neo Confucian Writings* (New York: Columbia University Press, 1963). Abbr.: CSL.

⁶ Ching, *Wisdom*, 108.

⁷ Mencius said: "If men [a person] suddenly see a child about to fall into a well, they will without exception experience a feeling of alarm and commiseration. *They will feel so*, not as a ground on which they may seek the praise of their neighbors and friends, nor from a dislike to the reputation of having been unmoved by such a thing." (*Mencius*, 2A:6; trans., James Legge, *The Chinese Classics*, v. 2 [New York: Paragon Books, 1966], 78)

Mencius stipulated four moral principles in the primordial human nature: commiseration, modesty and deference, shame and dislike, and approving and disapproving; see ibid. These are also called the Four Beginnings; see Yi Hwang's "Diagram of the Saying 'the Mind Combines and Governs the Nature and the Feelings," Kalton, *Sage*, 123-24. For Yang-ming's comment on the feeling of commiseration, see CSL:272.

⁸ Hitoyuki Iki characterized *liang-chih* as a revelation, which is "neither knowledge nor ignorance." See his "Wang Yang-ming's Doctrine of Innate Knowledge of the Good," *Philosophy East and West* 11 (1961), 27-44, esp. 41-42.

⁹ Ching, *Wisdom*, 108. Ching distinguished *liang-chih* from the Kantian notion of the "categorical imperative" as the means of discovery. Whereas the categorical imperative was discovered by an analytical examination of common knowledge, *liang-chih* was acquired through an intuitive experience of inner enlightenment.

¹⁰ In Chan's translation, "innate knowledge" signifies *liang-chih*.

¹¹ Tu Wei-ming, *Confucian Thought: Selfhood as Creative Transformation* (Albany: State University of New York Press, 1985), 32.

[12] Philip Ivanhoe, *Ethics in the Confucian Tradition: The Thought of Mencius and Wang Yang-ming* (Atlanta: Scholars Press, 1990), 103.

[13] *Hsiang-shan ch'üan-chi*, recited from Ivanhoe, 104.

[14] Ibid.

[15] Martin Heidegger identified the threefold structure of interpretation as *Vorhabe* ("forehaving" or "a taken-for-granted background"), *Vorsicht* ("fore-sight"), and *Vorgriff* ("fore-conception"). This fore-structure of interpretation raises the problem of the hermeneutical circle, where all interpreting is necessarily circular. See Heidegger, *Being and Time*, trans. John Macquarie and Edward Robinson (Harper & Row, c. 1962), 191-195.

[16] I use this Bultmannian term in a broader definition. Here the demythologization does means not only a scientific interpretation but also other interpretive attempts "to recover the deeper meaning behind the mythological [and traditionally mystified] conceptions." See Rudolf Bultmann, *Jesus Christ and Mythology* (New York: Charles Scribner's Son, 1958), 3.

[17] From Wang's poem, *"Four Hymns to Liang Chih Shown to My Students, in Wang Wen-ch'eng-kung ch'üan-shu* 20:629a, recited from Ivanhoe, 109.

[18] Wang said in *"Shu Wei Shih-meng chüan,"* "The knowledge of the good *(liang-chih)* which is [present] in the mind and heart may be called sagehood *(sheng);"* recited from Ching, *Wisdom*, 113.

[19] Legge, *Chinese Classics*, V. 1, 248.

[20] See *Chan Wing-tsit, A Source Book in Chinese Philosophy* (Princeton: Princeton University Press, 1963), 566.

[21] See *ibid., 600-602.*

[22] *Dasein* literally means "there is." Heidegger defined the term: "[T]o work out the question of being adequately, we must make an entity [being]--the inquirer--transparent in his own being. . . . This entity [being] which each of us is himself and which includes inquiring as one of the possibilities of its Being, we shall denote by the term Dasein," *Being and Time*, 27. Similar to Wang, Heidegger also rejected traditional (Cartesian and Husserlian) distinctions of the Western philosophy such as mental content and independent object, subject and object, immanent and transcendent, representation and represented, conscious and unconscious, explicit and tacit, reflective and unreflective.

Julia Ching compared *hsin-chih-pen-t'i* to the *Dasein*; see Ching, *Wisdom*, note, 112. Tu also tried to establish a Neo-Confucian ontology in a dialogue with this notion; see Tu's article, "Neo-Confucian Ontology: A Preliminary Questioning," *Confucian Thought*, 149-170.

[23] See Chang Tsai, *Correcting Youthful Ignorance*; Chan, *Source Book*, 501.

[24] See Ching, *Wisdom*, 145.

[25] See Tu, "Subjectivity and Ontological Reality--An Interpretation of Wang Yang-ming's Mode of Thinking," in *Humanity and Self-Cultivation: Essays in Confucian Thought* (Berkeley: Asian Humanities Press, 1979), 138-61. This section relies on Tu's interpretation.

[26] See ibid., 156, 159; also *Confucian Thought*, 33.

[27] Tu, *Humanity*, 156.

[28] Webster's New Universal Unabridged Dictionary, 2nd. ed., 1486.

[29] Tu, *Humanity*, 156.

[30] Ibid.

[31] Chan, *Instructions*, 272.

[32] Tu, *Humanity*, 157.

[33] Tu, *Confucian Thought*, 33.

[34] Chan, *Source Book*, 497-498.

[35] For general discussions on this cardinal notion of Confucianism, see Chan Wing-tsit, "The Evolution of the Confucian Concept Jen," *Neo-Confucianism Etc.: Essays by Wing-tsit Chan* (Hong Kong: Oriental Society, 1969), 1-44.

[36] See Peter A. Boodberg, *"The Semasiology of Some Primary Confucian Concepts," Philosophy East and West* 2:4 (1953), 329-30.

[37] Chan, *Instructions*, 272

[38] Humanity *(jen)* also means "seed."

[39] Chu Hsi revised the term to "renovating the people" *(hsin-min)*. But Wang argued for the original rendition, "loving the people." See Chan, *Instructions.*, 276.

[40] Ibid., 273-74. Italics are mine.

[41] CSL: 56f.. Cf. Ching, *Wisdom*, 129.

[42] For Neo-Confucian concept of human being, see Tu's article, "The Neo-Confucian Concept of Man," in *Humanity*, 71-82.

[43] Ching, *Wisdom*, 145.

[44] See *Boodberg*, 327-29.

⁴⁵ Iki designated the master-servant relationship between *liang-chih* and human beings; see "Wang . . .," 43.

⁴⁶ CSL: 257, revised; cf. Ching, *Wisdom*, 145.

⁴⁷ Karl Barth, *Church Dogmatics, Vol. IV, 2* (Edinburgh: T. & T. Clark, 1958). Abbr.: IV/2.

⁴⁸ As T. F. Torrance corrected in the Preface of CD IV/1, the German word *Versöhnung* for Barth includes both atonement and reconciliation in English. However, the translator, Bromiley translated it as atonement throughout the volumes. However, reconciliation is the more appropriate English term, because when Barth said *Versöhnung*, it has a more inclusive meaning than traditional atonement theories. See CD IV/1, vii.

⁴⁹ For Barth's doctrine of the Trinity, see Claude Welch, *In This Name: The Doctrine of the Trinity in Contemporary World* (New York: Charles Scribner's Sons, 1952); also Eberhard Jüngel, *The Doctrine of the Trinity: God's Being is in Becoming* (Grand Rapids: Wm B. Eerdmans Publishing Co., 1976); for its criticism, Jürgen Moltmann, *The Trinity and the Kingdom: the Doctrine of God*, trans. Magaret Kohl (San Francisco: Harper & Row, Publishers, 1981), esp. 139-144.

⁵⁰ Barth said, "as man He can open the frontier, not to make man a second God, but as man, by Himself becoming and being man, to set him within this frontier, to bring him to His own home, to place him in and with Himself at the side of the Father (Jn. 1:1-2)" (IV/2: 44).

⁵¹ Barth said, "It does this *a posteriori*, with a reference to Him, to the Son of God actually existing in the flesh. It does not derive from a known *a priori*, a superior possibility, but only from the given actuality, from Him Himself." (IV/2: 62)

⁵² Barth said, "Wherever there is knowledge of Jesus Christ, it takes place in the power of His witness, in the mystery and miracle, the outpouring and receiving, of the gift of the Holy Spirit" (IV/2: 126).

⁵³ See Robert McAfee Brown, *Gustavo Gutiérrez: An Introduction to Liberation Theology* (Maryknoll: Orbis Books, 1990), 57-74.

⁵⁴ Barth said, "Jesus was not in any sense a reformer championing new orders against the old ones . . . He did not represent or defend or champion any programme--whether political, economic, moral or religious, whether conservative or progressive" (IV/2: 171).

⁵⁵ Such a unity of word and deed is identical with the etymological connotation of the Chinese character, *ch'eng* (sincerity). The Chinese character *ch'eng* consists of two graphs that mean word (or speech) and

accomplishment (action); etymologically, it denotes a sincere actualization of one's word. The life-act of royal humanity manifests a paradigm of *ch'eng*, i.e., the sincere being and becoming in the unity of speaking and acting. See "A Confucian Interpretation of Christ," in the last section.

[56] Karl Barth, *Church Dogmatics, Vol. III, 2*, ed by G. W. Bromiley and T. F. Torrance, trans. Harold Knight, et. al. (Edinburgh: T. & T. Clark, 1960). Abbr.: III/2.

[57] Stuart D. McLean, *Humanity in the Thought of Karl Barth* (Edinburgh: T. & T. Clark, 1981), 29.

[58] Ibid., 31.

[59] Barth said:
> "If 'God for humanity' is the eternal covenant revealed and effective in time in the humanity of Jesus, in this decision of the Creator for the creature there arises a relationship that is not alien to the Creator, to God as God, but we might almost say appropriate and natural to Him. God repeats in this relationship *ad extra* a relationship proper to Himself in His inner divine essence. Entering into this relationship, He makes a copy of Himself. Even in His inner divine being there is relationship. To be sure, God is One in Himself. But He is not alone. There is in Him a co-existence, co-inherence and reciprocity. God in Himself is not just simple, but in the simplicity of His essence He is threefold--the Father, the Son and the Holy Ghost. He posits Himself, is posited by Himself, and confirms Himself in both respects, as His own origin and also as His own goal. . . . and in this triunity He is the original and source of every I and Thou, of the I which is eternally from and to the Thou and therefore supremely I. And it is this relationship in the inner divine being which is repeated and reflected in God's eternal covenant with human being as revealed and operative in time in the humanity of Jesus. (III/2, 218f.)

[60] John D. Godsey, ed., *Karl Barth's Table Talks* (Richmond: John Knox, 1962), 57.

[61] Barth said, "We gladly see and are seen; we gladly speak and listen; we gladly receive and offer assistance" (III/2: 265).

[62] Barth differentiated the nature of humanity as the joyful being-in-togetherness from Christian love (*agape*). In doing so, he accomplishes two things. On the one hand, he resisted theomonistic theologians' frequent custom to devalue the authenticity of humanity in contrast with Christian love. On the other hand, he put two important themes--the ontology of humanity (theological anthropology) and the Christian freedom to be fully human (sanctification)--in their proper places. This is precisely why he dealt with the freedom of human being as joyful co-humanity in the context of the doctrine of Creation (III), and with Christian love in the context of the

doctrine of Reconciliation (IV/2). However, when he treated Christian love, he did not make such a sharp distinction between natural humanity and Christian love.

[63] Barth's definition of humanity as being-in-encounter, being-in-togetherness, or *Mitmenschlichkeit* renders a remarkable parallelism to the Confucian notion of *jen* that etymologically has the twofold meaning of both human and co-humanity. Barth seemed to have known that Confucius (and Martin Buber) formulated humanity in a similar relational model (see the last section). However, Barth differentiated his understanding as a purely theological viewpoint. Nevertheless, there is no actual difference at the point of seeing humanity as co-humanity between Barth's Christian understanding of humanity in the image of God--*Mitmenschlichkeit*--and the Confucian notion of humanity in the *jen*-paradigm. Barth also said, "What we have called humanity can be present and known in varying degrees of perfection or imperfection even where there can be no question of a direct revelation and knowledge of Jesus Christ. This reality of human nature and its recognition are not, therefore, restricted to the Christian community . . ." (III/2: 276)

[64] Tu, *Humanity*, 156.

[65] The election of God through salvation history also has a dimension of immanent-transcendence. However, it basically grounds on radical transcendence and focuses on its historical immanence.

[66] See Tu, *Humanity*, 139.

[67] See Paul Tillich, *Systematic Theology*, Vol. I (Chicago: The University of Chicago Press, 1951), 259.

[68] See Jean Sangbae Ri, *Confucius et Jesus Christ: La Premiere Theologie Chretienne en Coree D'apres L'oeuvre de Yi Piek lettre Confuceen 1754-1786* (Paris: Editions Beauchesne, 1979). Also Yun, *Han'gukjok Sinhak: Song ui Haesokhak [The Korean Theology: Hermeneutics of Sincerity]* (Seoul: Son Myung Munhwasa, 1972)

[69] See Hans Küng, *Theology for the Third Millennium: An Ecumenical View*, trans. by Peter Heinegg (New York: Doubleday, 1988); also Zhang Longxi, "The Tao and Logos: Notes on Derrida's Critique of Logocentricism," *Critical Inquiry* (March 1985), 385-398.

[70] J. Moltmann, *The Way of Jesus Christ: Christology in Messianic Dimensions*, trans. by Margaret Kohl (San Francisco: Harper, 1990).

[71] Ibid., xiv.

[72] Ibid., xv.

[73] See Tu Wei-ming, *Centrality and Commonality: An Essay on Confucian Religiousness*, rev. ed. (Albany: State Univ. of New York Press, 1989), 102-107.

Chapter Three

Imago Dei and *T'ien-ming*: John Calvin Meets Yi T'oegye

Korean Christianity is distinctive in the fact that, among traditionally Confucian societies, Korea is both the most Christianized (at least in population) and the most Confucianized (at least in form) country. Hence, a Confucian-Christian dialogue is crucial for Korean society and constitutive of doing Korean Christian theology for the 21st century. A dialogue between the teachings of Yi T'oegye (1501-70)[1] and John Calvin (1509-64) is particularly significant in this context, because their legacies have made the most far-reaching influences in the Korean formation of Confucianism and Christianity.

On the one hand, Korean Neo-Confucianism was firmly established by T'oegye, and his school of the Way had played decisive roles in the trajectory of Korean Confucianism. On the other hand, Presbyterianism (or the Reformed tradition), founded by Calvin, has exceptionally flourished ever since it was introduced into this country. The Korean Presbyterian Church has been not only the largest in total membership but also culturally and socially the most active among all Christian denominations in Korea. Within the history of a little more than a century, furthermore, it has grown to be the largest in membership among all the Reformed churches in the world, even surpassing the size of the American Presbyterian churches that have made major contribution to plant the church in Korea. In Korea, the Reformed tradition has achieved a miracle, perhaps the most successful mission in its entire history.[2]

Calvin and T'oegye, two contemporaneous figures of the 16th Century, lived in two radically different worlds; namely, Christendom and Confucendom. Nevertheless, their lives and thoughts present remarkable similarities that, I think, illuminate some important clues for the great success of Presbyterianism in Korea. Interestingly, both of them wrote two seminal treatises to crystallize their traditions; Calvin's *Institutes of Christian Religion* (1559)[3] and T'oegye's *Ten Diagrams of Sage Learning* (1568).[4] Moreover, both of these writings were originally written to explain the essences of their religions to their kings. Calvin wrote the *Institutes* to defend his religion to Francis I: T'oegye drew the *Ten Diagrams* to educate Sŏnjo.

Christianity and Confucianism originate from two radically different religious visions what I call 'theohistorical' (salvation history) and 'anthropocosmic' (the unity of humanity and cosmos).[5] Since the two paradigms have mutually divergent foci (roughly, theism and humanism), their *a priori* dimensions such as the Christian God and the Confucian Heaven are not adequate starting points for a genuine dialogue. Rather, since Christianity and Confucianism meet each other in the common issue of humanity ('the common quest for the *Tao* of full humanity'), humanity is a more legitimate point of departure for a practical and productive dialogue.[6]

The Confucian-Christian dialogue I formulated previously between Wang Yang-ming and Karl Barth vindicates thick resemblances between Confucianism and Christianity on the issue of humanization--how to be fully human--despite their radical differences.[7] This Confucian-Christian dialogue I am now attempting between Calvin and T'oegye also presents striking resemblances, even thicker than those between Wang and Barth. Below, I will juxtapose some of the 'similarities-in-differences' which I find striking in a dialogue between Calvin and T'oegye on the theme of humanity.[8]

1. Original Humanity: *Imago Dei* and *T'ien-ming*

Calvin and T'oegye are same in a belief that human beings are relational to and inseparably intertwined with the transcendent grounds of being (namely, God and Heaven).

Hence, their anthropologies are basically relational and transcendental. The Christian doctrine of Imago Dei *(the image of God) and the Neo-Confucian concept of* T'ien-ming *(Heavenly endowment) reveal saliently this characteristic of a relational and transcendental anthropology. Calvin and T'oegye are same in defining humanity as a mirror or a microcosm to image and reflect the glory and the goodness of the transcendent ground of being. Moreover, they are remarkably similar in understanding attributes of the goodness endowed in original humanity. Calvin described them as wisdom, virtue, justice, and holiness; in short, integrity and rectitude: T'oegye expressed the attributes of the original nature as benevolence* (jen), *righteousness* (i), *propriety* (li), *and wisdom* (chih); *in short, sincerity* (ch'eng) *and principle* (li). *If the idiosyncratic differences between God and Heaven are bracketed, the understandings of Calvin and T'oegye on ontological humanity seem to be almost mutually interchangeable.*

1) Relational Anthropology:

The knowledge of humanity and the knowledge of God are the two basic themes of Christian theology. In fact, Calvin was very explicit in asserting that anthropology is as important as theology.[9] The *Institutes* is written not only for the true doctrine of God but also for the true doctrine of humanity as the subject of faith. Brian Gerrish said well, "nothing less than the whole of the *Institutes* is required to set out his doctrine of man,[10] just as the work *as a whole* presents his doctrine of God."[11] In Calvin's theology, hence, anthropology and theology are relational, "inseparably intertwined," and "mutually condition each other."[12]

The Confucian understanding of humanity is also closely related to Heaven. It is not much to say that, in the confuciology of T'oegye, the relationship of Heaven and humanity is more primary than that of *li* (principle) and *ch'i* (material force), a subject at which T'oegye is famous. In fact, the Four-Seven Debates, "the most celebrated and important controversy in Korean Neo-Confucian history,"[13] began with T'oegye's revision of *the Diagram of Heavenly Endowment* drawn by Chŏng Chi-un (1509-61) which defines humanity as a being that illuminates and reveals Heaven (Heavenly endowment). T'oegye's understanding of human's intimate relationship with Heaven is not so much mechanistic nor metaphysical as personal, using the metaphor of a wider family.[14] This familial relationship is well expressed in *the Western Inscription* of Chang Tsai (1020-77): "Heaven is my father and Earth is my mother." Because of this significance, T'oegye included this *Western Inscription* as the second diagram in his *Ten Diagrams*.[15]

2) *Imago Dei* and *T'ien-ming*:

Just as the Genesis states that the first two human beings were created in the image of God (Gen. 1: 27), *The Doctrine of the Mean*, says, "What Heaven imparts (*T'ien-ming*) to man is called human nature."[16] Just as the doctrine of *imago Dei* is the center of Calvin's theological anthropology, the teaching of *T'ien-ming* is the heart of T'oegye's Neo-Confucian anthropology. Both doctrines state very explicitly that humanity is relational to and inseparably intertwined with its transcendent ontological ground.

In the confuciology of T'oegye, the *Diagram of T'ien-ming* refers to an epistemological process to knowing the origin of creation through the created human beings and natural things (i.e., a perspective from the below), while the *Diagram of T'ai-chi (the Great Ultimate)* explains the metaphysical process of creation from the origin (i.e., from the above).[17] Similarly, the theology of Calvin also has a twofold structure; the doctrine of *imago Dei* is certainly a perspective from the below, if the doctrine of the Triune God is a perspective from the above.

Calvin called the *imago Dei* "a heavenly image" or "celestial image," a precise translation of *T'ien-ming*. He favored using the metaphor of a mirror, a reflection, to explain the image of God.[18] While the whole of creation is a theater that vindicates the glorious work of God, human being is "distinguished from the mute creation by his ability to reflect God's glory in a conscious response of thankfulness" like the brightest mirror.[19] According to the *Diagram of T'ien-ming*, likewise, while the myriad things in the cosmos are made of *T'ien-ming*, human being is the only specie that illuminates and discloses the goodness of Heaven in a sufficient purity and transparency like a brilliant mirror.[20]

Further, Calvin and T'oegye are strikingly similar in their understanding of original humanity. Just as original humanity (*hsing*), a heavenly endowment, was perfect, the image of God implanted in original humanity implies "the perfection of our whole nature. . . as appeared when Adam was endued with a right judgment, had affections in harmony with reason, had all his sense sound and well regulated, and truly excelled in everything good."[21] Calvin called this perfect condition of humanity *integrity*: "The integrity with which Adam was endowed is expressed by this word [*imago*] . . . truly referred his excellence to exceptional gifts bestowed upon him by his Maker."[22] T'oegye called this perfect condition sincerity which includes four "constant characteristics of the *Tao* of Heaven"; origination, flourishing, benefiting, and firmness (*yüan, heng, li, chen*).[23]

Calvin also called the original order of humanity rectitude (*rectitudo*). The image of God contains not only the external goodness (*bonum adventium*) but also the internal goodness (*bonum interim*): "The likeness must be within, in himself. It must be something which is not external to him, but is properly the internal good of the soul."[24] Calvin described the characteristics of this internal goodness as "wisdom, virtue, justice, and holiness."[25] The school of *Hsing-li*, to which T'oegye faithfully attached himself, identifies original humanity (*hsing*) with principle (*li*). Since Heavenly endowment is identified with *li*, humanity is viewed in unity with Heaven through the same *li*. In correspondence to the four constant characteristics of the Tao of Heaven, Neo-Confucianism designates four attributes of original humanity as benevolence (*jen*), righteousness (*i*), propriety (*li*), and wisdom (*chih*). These four beginnings strikingly resonate with Calvin's characterizations of the internal goodness of original humanity; wisdom, virtue, justice, and holiness.

Furthermore, for Calvin, the creation of both Adam and Eve according to the image of God means that human is basically a "social animal"[26] and that humanity is created to "cultivate mutual society between themselves."[27] The etymological meaning of *jen* is co-humanity (two humans). Hence, long before Karl Barth, Calvin already accepted fully the Confucian equation that the root-paradigm of humanity is co-humanity, or being-in-togetherness.[28] Confucius said that reciprocity (*shu*) is a consistent principle of Confucianism. Calvin also underscored that the *imago*-relation specially implies the "sacred bond and mutual reciprocity" which a person has to do with God, fellow human beings, and natural things.

For Calvin, moreover, the "express image of God" is Christ, the Son of God who faithfully obeyed the Father until the crucifixion on the cross. Calvin regarded filial piety as "the subject basis of the image."[29] Hence, not only in Confucianism but also in Calvin's theology, the paradigm of humanity is described as a filial relation of the Son to the Father in Heaven through the story of the Trinity.

Calvin advocated that, by the *imago*-relation, a person could participate in the order of God. To be truly human refers to recovering the whole humanity (integrity) and original order (rectitude). Calvin said, after all, "regeneration is nothing else than the restoration of the same image."[30] Likewise, T'oegye affirmed that, by the endowment-relation, a person could participate in the principle of Heaven. To be fully human means recovering the whole human nature (*ch'eng*) and the original cosmic pattern (*li*). Except the idiosyncratic differences between God and Heaven, the teachings of Calvin and T'oegye on original humanity seem to be strikingly similar and almost mutually interchangeable.

2. Existential Humanity: Fallen Nature and Human Mind

Calvin and T'oegye are same in perceiving the mind-and-heart (hsin) *as the primary locus of original humanity. They agreed that the mind-and-heart in reality, however, is so ambivalent and vulnerable that it functions ambiguously against its original goodness. Accordingly, both of them made a distinction between original humanity with the original goodness (ontological humanity) and actual humanity in ambiguity and ambivalence (existential humanity). In theology, it is expressed as a sharp distinction between original humanity first created by God and actual humanity after the Fall. In confuciology, it is indicated as a dichotomy between the mind of Tao* (Tao-hsin) *and the human mind* (jen-hsin). *Consequently, how to recover and restore the original goodness immanent in ontological humanity beyond the ambivalent and dualistic nature of existential humanity becomes the primary subject matter for both of them. This primary project of humanization, i.e., a learning how to restore true and full humanity, is expressed in the doctrines of sanctification and self-cultivation (sage learning) respectively.[31] It is true that Calvin defended the doctrine of original sin and rigorously scrutinized the negative reality of corrupted humanity, whereas T'oegye carefully investigated the phenomena of mind-and-heart. If we look deeper into their thoughts, however, we can find that the differences in their analyses of human reality are not so thick but subtle. As T. F. Torrance pointed out correctly, the doctrines of original sin and total depravity should not be understood independently but as corollaries to the doctrines of Grace and Christology. T'oegye's view of human mind-and-heart is not so romantic, as much as he experienced four bloody purges among Confucian literati in one of which his beloved brother was killed. Moreover, they converge in a comprehension of humanity's existential ambiguities as arising from a distortion and perversion of original goodness, rejecting the ontological status of evil.*

1) Ambivalent Human Condition

Calvin did not make a radical dichotomy between mind (soul) and heart (body). Rational portraits of modern Calvinism are excessive and incorrect from the vantage point of the historical Calvin.[32] Calvin said, "the chief seat of the divine image is in his mind and heart where it was eminent."[33] He seems to be very much in agreement with Confucianism in a belief that the *locus* of human's transcendental relationship lies not in the mind (reason) alone, differentiating from the body, but in the mind-and-heart, a psychosomatic totality. The mind-and-heart (*hsin*) is a unique East Asian notion that transcends the body-and-soul dualism. T'oegye is famous with his insightful analysis on the nature and phenomena of the mind-and-heart (see *Diagrams* 6-8).

Calvin told twofold knowledge of humanity in correspondence to the twofold knowledge of God as Creator and Redeemer. In the *Institutes*, he first treated what original humanity was like when created (*Inst.*, 1.15), and then what human condition looks like since the fall (*Inst.*, 2.1-5). Gerrish summarized: "The existence of man in the design of God is defined by thankfulness, the correlate of God's goodness; the existence of man in sin is defined by pride or self-love, the antithesis of God's goodness."[34] Deeply conscious of the dualistic nature between ontological humanity and existential humanity, Calvin rigorously investigated the depth and complexity of human psyche long before S. Freud. His famous doctrine of depravity was formulated to explain such an ambivalent human condition, while remedying the problem of theodicy.

Calvin's discussion on humanity continued in the sections on Christology (the perfect humanity) and Christian life, which he spent much more pages to cover. Since the restoration of humanity "has dogmatic precedence even over the doctrine of the original state," it is not too much to say that humanization (sanctification) is the main agenda for Calvin's anthropology.

T'oegye perceived that the mind-and-heart as the master of the self is the nucleus of humanity, and the problematique of the mind-and-heart was the central issue of T'oegye's thought. Although he did not speak of the doctrine of depravity like Calvin, as a person who experienced four bloody 'literati purges,' T'oegye fully recognized the ambivalent vulnerability of human mind-and-heart in reality.[35] To explain this ambiguity, he developed further subtle Neo-Confucian distinctions between the mind of *Tao* and the human mind, before it is aroused and after it has been aroused, principle (*li*) and material force (*ch'i*), and original humanity (*hsing*) and feelings (*ch'ing*).

In the unity with the body, the mind-and-heart functions freely in the universe with no limitation of time and space. However, this capacity before it is aroused can be disturbed after it has been aroused. The substance (*t'i*) of the mind-and-heart before aroused is called original humanity, and its function (*yung*) after aroused is recognized as feelings.[36] The title of his *Diagram* 6 is "The mind-and-heart unites *li* and *ch'i*, and governs nature and feelings." The subtleties of their distinction and the nuance of their balance are the basic issue in his famous Four-Seven Debates with Ki Taesŭng (1529-92).

2) The Fallen Nature and the Human Mind

As T. F. Torrance argued, Calvin's doctrine of human depravity was not composed for a dogmatic purpose but for a didactic purpose in the context of the doctrine of Grace. "Calvin's doctrine of the fall of man and sin is a corollary of the doctrine of grace in forgiveness and salvation."[37] However, later Calvinist theologies unfortunately turned these Calvin's didactic devices into dogmatic procedure, and produced the doctrine of the fall and of human depravity without the context of grace. Interpreting grace as God's answer to human depravity is in fact an insult to the Creator. Torrance said:

> In actual fact, he [Calvin] refused to advance any doctrine of man, apart from God's original intention of grace in creating in the image of God, and apart from god's supreme act of grace in Jesus Christ for our salvation. Within these two brackets, and only within these two brackets, does Calvin give us an account of man's fallen nature and his sin. Never does he attempt to give a philosophical account of man's depravity.[38]

When Calvin said that a human being is completely despoiled of the spiritual image, it does not mean that the gifts naturally endowed are polluted or destroyed ontologically. "Sin does not mean an ontological break with God, for Calvin does not hold a doctrine of evil as the privation of being."[39] Even after the Fall, a human being is still a rational creature with a mind and a will that can reflect the image of God. Although we are utterly deprived of God's glory in rectitude, righteousness, and love, our natural gifts still remain. Although grievously impaired, we can see God's workmanship in our mind-and-heart that reflects God's image and distinguish between good and evil. In the mind-and-heart, there still remains 'a spark of knowledge,' 'a portion of light,' or 'a seed of religion.'[40]

Calvin's doctrine of justification by faith alone also does not deny the existence of natural goodness in the fallen humanity. But the righteousness with which sinners are clothed is not of their own but of Christ Himself, "the very image of God." "The more he presumes upon the relic of the *imago Dei* within him, the deeper he gets into the abyss of darkness and corruption and death. If the light that is in him is darkness, how great is that darkness!"[41]

Torrance emphasized repeatedly that Calvin's doctrine of total perversity must be interpreted in the context of his doctrine of the dynamic relation of human and God. "Total perversity thus means that man's personal being, grounded by grace in a continuous relation with the living God, has been perverted into an existence in which he is continually turned away from God, so that all that he does in the exercise of his God-given gifts is against God."[42] Hence, human has lost all rectitude (the divine order in creation) and is governed by a perverted order (*Inst.* 1.15.7). The whole order of creation has been perverted as a consequence of the fall of humanity.

Sin cannot destroy the image of God, but can pervert the whole (1.15.1; 2.1.9). "The total perversion of the mind or the reason means that the whole inclination of the mind is in the direction of alienation from God."[43] Calvin called the perverse motion in the mind *concupiscence*,[44] that is the 'wantonness and prurience of the human mind' (2.12.5). He also described concupiscence as 'the violent lawless movements which war with the order of God,' as 'a perpetual disorder and excess apparent in all our actions,' or as an 'inordinate desire' (3.3.12). Torrance defined, "*concupiscentia* is diametrically opposed to the *imago Dei* which reflects the order of God in creation. It is through this *unorderly dealing* that the creation is perverted, and God's glory diminished."[45] Concupiscence resonates with selfish desires, a Neo-Confucian notion 'diametrically opposed' to *T'ien-ming*, which will be explained later.

T'oegye viewed feelings as the function that issue from the substance of original humanity in the mind-and-heart.[46] Since the mind-and-heart is also a unity of *li* and *ch'i*, the issued feelings consist in two kinds. One which exposes purely the *li* of original humanity is called the four beginnings; namely, commiseration, modesty and deference, shame and dislike, and approving and disapproving. The other in which the *li* of original humanity is perturbed by the physical disposition is called the seven feelings; namely, joy, anger, grief, fear, love, hate, and desire.

After the series of debates with Ki Taesŭng, T'oegye changed his position to conclude that the four beginnings are what *li* issues and *ch'i* follows, whereas the seven feelings are what *ch'i* issues and *li* mounts it.[47] In other words, *li* issues primarily in the four beginnings, while *ch'i* does principally in the seven feelings. This demarcation is precisely to discern and establish a boundary line with the possibility of evil by the concrete grasp of the foundation of goodness.

T'oegye suggested the substance and function of the mind-and-heart in terms of the empty and spiritual and the knowing and perceiving. The empty and spiritual signifies the numinous capacity of knowing and perceiving when the mind-and-heart is empty by the invisible *li*. The empty and spiritual substance of the mind-and-heart appears as the knowing and perceiving (*Diagram* 6-b). He defined the spiritual and intelligence (*shen-ming*) as a totality that unites the substance and function of human mind-and-heart (*Diagram* 8). The spiritual and intelligence of the mind-and-heart is basically same as those of Heaven, and the mind-and-heart possesses the same spiritual and intelligence of Heaven.

Based on the *Diagram of the Mind-and-Heart* of Ch'eng Lin-yin,[48] T'oegye further classified six kinds of the mind-and-heart; namely, the original mind, the naturally good mind, the mind of the infant, the mind of the great person, the mind of *Tao*, and the human mind. The naturally good mind is the 'goodness endowed from Heaven.' The original mind is the 'originally inborn goodness.' The mind of the infant is pure and has no falsehood. But the mind of the great person is not only pure and has no falsehood, but also is conversant to all kinds of circumstances. In contrast to the naïve mind of the infant baby, the mind of the great person reveals the mature and accomplished mind of sage. This distinction entrenches the need of self-cultivation.

Especially, the polarity of the human mind and the mind of *Tao* is important. It uncovers the original source of the mind-and-heart and entails the foundation of human morality and the practice of self-cultivation. Whereas the human mind issues from the form of material force, the mind of *Tao* is based on the natural endowment, though they are mutually interrelated rather than clearly divided.[49] While the human mind consists in the impartiality of one's body, the mind of *Tao* reveals the commandment of Heaven. The former can be united with the latter only after a hearing of the commandment of the latter. Nevertheless, since sages also possess the human mind, we must distinguish between the human mind before fallen into evil and human desires that reveal the state of evil.[50]

T'oegye delineated the phenomena of good and evil arising with the issuance of the mind-and-heart in terms of *li* and *ch'i*. "That which *li* exposes and *ch'i* adjusts accordingly is good: that which *li* is hid by the hindrance of *ch'i* is evil."[51] On the one hand, the good arises when *li* becomes predominant in the mind-and-heart and *ch'i* adjusts itself obediently. On the other hand, the evil arises when *ch'i* becomes predominant and *li* is concealed by the blocking of *ch'i*. *Li* as the source of good is a pure goodness, whereas *ch'i* as the source of evil is a condition in which good and evil divide. *Li* refers to the standard for human living, i.e., the Heavenly Principle that was endowed in original humanity and still is immanent in the mind-and-heart. *Ch'i* implies the physical disposition, a basis in which human mind and body consist. A person actualizes the good when the Heavenly Principle is disclosed brilliantly in one's being beyond the physical disposition, whereas one falls into the evil when the Heavenly Principle is concealed by the physical disposition. Hence, T'oegye's doctrines of *li* and *ch'i* do not refer essentially to a system of metaphysical speculation, but signifies a moral principle of self-cultivation to preserve and disclose the Heavenly Principle and to restrain human desires beyond the physical disposition.

In the *Explanation of the Diagram of* T'ien-ming, T'oegye said, "the will makes the mind-and-heart arise, embraces and impels the feeling to the left or to the right, or to follow the justice of the Heavenly Principle, or to the partiality of human desires. The distinction of good and evil is made from this. This implies the so called 'the incipient wellsprings divide good and evil.'"[52] The division of good and evil appears more vividly in the will, issuing spontaneously from the mind-and-heart, than in the feeling, issuing responsively. The good is an innate thing, because it originates from the pure goodness of the nature, whereas evil is a secondary thing arising by the blocking of the physical disposition. T'oegye denied the actuality of evil, succeeding Cheng-i's definition that evil is "what surpasses or is unattainable."[53]

The division of good and evil involves in the subtlest beginning of issuance, i.e., the incipient wellsprings. A distinction of good and evil and a choice of good should be made from the point when the willing and the knowing begin to arise. However, the division of good and evil does not denote such an opposition as *yin* and *yang* arise to divide from the Great Ultimate (*T'ai-chi*). Evil does not originate from original humanity and cannot be an ontological substance equal to the good. According to T'oegye, evil is not an ontological being, but an existential thing that arises from the disturbance of the physical disposition. Therefore, T'oegye and Calvin are same in a perception that evil is not an innate or original being.

3. The Restoration of Original Humanity: Sanctification and Self-cultivation

*For both Calvin and T'oegye, reverence (*pietas *and* ching*) is the central concept that permeates throughout their thoughts. For T'oegye, without doubt,* ching *is the cardinal concept of self-cultivation that involves a personal and corresponding relationship with the Lord of Heaven (*Shang-t'i*). For Calvin,* pietas *was "the shorthand symbol for his whole understanding and practice of Christian faith and life."*[54] *For both of them, reverence includes both fear and love (*mysterium tremendum et fascinas*) toward the ultimate ground of being and has a doctrinal precedence to knowledge (*doctrina *and* li*). T'oegye's overarching methodology of sage learning is the 'dwelling in the reverence and investigating the principle.' It is not too much to say that, though the object of investigation is different, Calvin holds structurally a same methodology, as faith-seeking-understanding (*fides quaerens intellectum*) is the classical definition of theology. Whereas* li *is the object of investigation for T'oegye (confuciology), Jesus Christ (the Word) is the object of faith for Calvin (theology). Furthermore, they converge in a belief that these objects of investigation are also the transcendent grounds of being which enable us to attain the* *radical humanity with original goodness. For* li *and Jesus Christ refer to the perfect manifestations of* T'ien-ming *and* imago Dei. *T'oegye also articulated this task in terms of the 're-embodying Heaven and progressing along the Way,' whereas Calvin explained it by the way of the restoring the original image of God through the faith in Christ and walking under the direction of the Holy Spirit. They are same in arguing for reverence as the inner means and righteousness as the outer means in order to achieve sanctification and self-cultivation. In a nutshell, sanctification is the realization of Christ (the perfect image of God) through hearing the Word (theology), and self-cultivation is the embodiment of* T'ien-ming *through investigating* li *(confuciology). If Christ (the Word) is identified with the principle* (li), *the structure of humanization in Calvin's theology and T'oegye's confuciology will be basically same; both of them point to sage learning.*

1) Calvin's Doctrine of Sanctification (*Pietas*):

Since the Christian Gospel speaks of human salvation in total terms, Calvin claimed, the doctrine of human depravity must be stated also in total terms. This logic applies also to the doctrine of the *imago Dei*. The Gospel tells us that we can be restored to a being in the image of God only by going outside of ourselves to Christ, who is "the expressed image of God." The revelation of grace inescapably infers that Christ (cf. *li*) is our righteousness (*i*), wisdom (*chih*), and *imago Dei* (*T'ien-ming*), whereas a fallen human being is quite bereft of the image of God.[55]

Knowing God and being in the image of God are closely interrelated. But we cannot use the image as a means of knowing God, because the image is only a reflex of the glory of God. We should not indulge in a speculative imagination to know God: "All knowledge of God, apart from His revelation, is a vast abyss that swallows up our thoughts in the thickest darkness. God is Himself the Author of all our knowledge of Him, while His Word is both the standard and the warrant of its Truth."[56] Calvin's emphasis upon the Word signifies that "*all our knowledge of God is essentially analogical, i.e., through a revelation which accommodates itself to the humble capacity of the human mind.*" Nevertheless, "*The relation between God and the analogical element is not ontological but essentially sacramental.*"[57] These analogical and visible elements have validity only in relation to the Word and the Spirit to convey the Truth.[58] They are only symbols made to point beyond themselves.[59] Any remnant of light formerly possessed cannot serve "as a predisposition for faith or as an analogical point of contact for the true knowledge of God."[60] The only preparation a person can do is to deny and empty oneself "objectively through the Cross, subjectively in *metanoia*."[61]

Calvin affirmed the inseparability between the two doctrines of justification and sanctification. They are a twofold fruit of the same faith:

> Why, then, are we justified by faith? Because by faith we grasp Christ's righteousness, by which alone we are reconciled to God. Yet you could not grasp this without at the same time grasping sanctification also... Therefore Christ justifies no one whom he does not at the same time sanctify. These benefits are joined together by an everlasting and indissoluble bond, so that those whom he illumines by his wisdom, he redeems; those whom he redeems, he justifies; those whom he justifies, he sanctifies. (*Inst.* 3. 16.1.)

While justification is the external imputation of righteousness, sanctification is the inner process of continual struggle under the direction of the Holy Spirit toward the restoration of the *imago Dei*. The purpose of sanctification is the restoration of a lost order through the restoration of the image of God in us. The work of Christ is precisely for this restoration of us to the original rectitude (*li*) by regenerating the image of God in Christ: "Christ is the most perfect image of God; if we are conformed to it, we are so restored that with true piety, righteousness, purity, and intelligence we bear God's image" (*Inst.* 1.15.4). Christians are no other than those who are elected and called to order and fulfill this harmonious structure of God's order through their participation.[62]

Calvin put a special emphasis on the term *pietas* (reverence or piety). *Pietas* is both "the predominant category of Calvin's spirituality" and "the shorthand symbol" for Calvin's whole understanding and practice of Christian faith and life.[63] Calvin attested that human beings are created for reverence. God has planted the awareness of divinity in our mind-and-heart and surrounded us with irresistible signs for the order of God. Reverence is "the attitude of a man being integrated within God's order: a pious person is one who has taken his place within God's order."[64]

In the *Institutes*, Calvin defined *pietas* as "reverence joined with the love of God which the knowledge of his benefits induces" (*Inst.* 1.2.1). Reverence is the root of love, and *pietas* takes the higher position than *caritas* (love), the cardinal Christian virtue. *Pietas* means the reverence of God (the first commandment), and *caritas* implies our just living among our neighbors (the second commandment). Calvin, like Confucians, assured that filial obedience is the foundation of reverence. For the first step to reverence is no other than "to know that God is a father to us" (*Inst.* 2.6.4). "*Pietas* bespeaks the walk of us adopted children of God the Father, adopted brothers and sisters of Christ the Son."[65] Battles put the interrelationship among the terms related to *pietas* in the following diagram.[66]

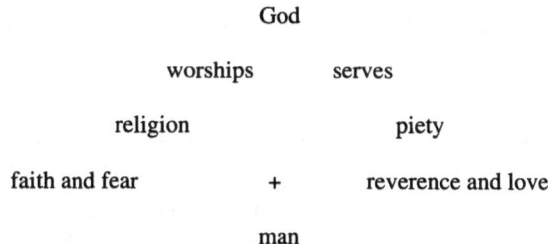

2) T'oegye's Teaching of Self-cultivation (*Ching*)

The basic methodology of T'oegye's sage learning is the 'dwelling in the reverence' and the 'investigating the principle.' These two methods consist of the two inseparable sides of one sage learning, mutually serving each other as "the outside and the inside" or as "the root and the branch." If the investigating the principle refers to an epistemology of knowing (*chih*), the dwelling in the reverence implies a doctrine of self-cultivation (*hsing*).

The 'investigating the principle' is to know and perceive *li* in everything and every event in one's life. It means a realization of *li* that is immanent in things as their order and principle by the ability of the knowing and perceiving, a function of the mind-and-heart. Since *li* is the substance of the mind-and-heart, we can know and perceive *li* latent in things: "*Li* and *ki* [*ch'i*] conjoin as the mind-and-heart, and it possesses as it were unfathomable emptiness and spirituality such that if things or affairs approach it is able to perceive them."[67]

The Great Learning suggests a specific method to investigate the principle of things, i.e., the 'investigation of things' and the 'extension of knowledge.' T'oegye explicated that the investigation of things is a process of learning in which, investigating *li* in depth, the mind-and-heart grows to attain knowledge. Before the debates with Ki Taesŭng, T'oegye held an epistemological position that the function of the knowing and perceiving in the mind-and-heart actively performs the investigation of the principle of things. After hearing Ki's argument that "*li* of itself approaches," however, he changed his position to accept that *li* manifests itself actively and that the mind-and-heart also waits passively for this approach of *li*.

T'oegye rejected Wang Yang-ming's doctrine of the unity of knowing and acting. Instinctive and sensual knowledge, based on the physical nature, can be attained without effort. However, since moral knowledge is grounded on the principle of righteousness, it cannot be obtained without learning and practice.[68] For this reason, T'oegye distinguished acting from knowing and proposed that knowing and acting mutually advance and reciprocally support each other "like two wheels or two wings."[69]

Ching is the center of T'oegye's teaching of self-cultivation. In the *Ten Diagrams*, he said, "these ten diagrams all take mindfulness as essential."[70] *Ching*, as the master of the mind-and-heart, is the nucleus by which the mind-and-heart is controlled and converged. In the "Diagram of the Study of the Mind-and-Heart," Ch'eng Fu-hsin explained (*Diagrams* 8):

> In sum, the essence of applying one's effort is nothing other than a matter of not departing from constant mindfulness [*ching*], for the mind is the master of the entire person and mindfulness is the master of the mind. If one who pursues learning will but thoroughly master what is meant by "focusing on one thing without departing from it," "becoming properly ordered and controlled, grave and quite," and "recollecting the mind and making it always awake and alert," his practice will be utterly perfect and complete, and entering the condition of sagehood likewise will not be difficult.[71]

The "focusing on one thing without departing from it" bespeaks of the state when the mind-and-heart is so concentrated and attentive as to be fully mindful. The structure of *ching* involves in the correspondingly harmonious relations among action and tranquility, substance and function, and in and out. When the mind-and-heart is not yet aroused (or in tranquility), "grave and quite" becomes the substance of *ching*. When the mind-and-heart has been aroused (or in action), "becoming properly ordered and controlled" becomes the function of *ching*.

For the practical method of *ching*, T'oegye paid a special interest in the quite-sitting, and combined the grave and quite mind with a quite posture of body. The learning of *ching* cannot be achieved at one time. It begins from the state of self-conscious attempts of "recollecting the mind and making it always awake and alert," and arrives at the state of perfection where one freely identifies one's mind-and-heart with the principle of the *Tao*.[72]

In the polarity of the mind of *Tao* and the human mind, T'oegye summed up the method of self-cultivation in terms of the 'blocking human desires and preserving Heavenly principle':

> In general, although the study of the mind-and-heart is complex, one can sum up its essence as nothing other than blocking [self-centered] human desires and preserving the principle of Heaven, just these two and that is all. . . . All the matters that are involved in blocking human desires should be categorized on the side of the human mind, and all that pertain to preserving the principle of Heaven should be categorized on the side of the mind of the Tao.[73]

The purpose of *ching* lies in attaining harmoniously corresponding relationships with other people and Heaven in the practice of everyday life. This learning leads us finally to obtain sagehood in the unity of Heaven and humanity, transcending the polarity of the mind of *Tao* and the human mind. T'oegye advised the king:

> The practice of this kind of reverent fear and mindfulness is nothing extraordinary; it is simply part of everyday life, but it can bring about the "perfect equilibrium [of the mind before it is aroused] and perfect harmony [after it is aroused," establish [heaven and earth] in their proper positions and accomplish the nurture [of all things]." Virtuous conduct is simply a matter of proper human relationships, but through it the wondrous unity of Heaven and man is attained.[74]

3) Sanctification and Self-cultivation

Christianity and Confucianism are normally contrasted: Whereas theology is based on the infusion or the imputation of the external and transcendental substance (the divinity of Christ), confuciology focuses on the revitalization of the dynamic relation with the internal and immanent source (*li*) through the practice of learning. To put it in their terms, whereas theology underscores justification (for salvation), confuciology focuses on self-cultivation (for sagehood).

However, the comparison of Calvin's theology and T'oegye's confuciology discloses that such a simple distinction does not say the whole truth. On the contrary, the differences between Reform Christianity and Neo-Confucianism represented by Calvin and T'oegye are not so thick but thin and subtle. Although in different terms, Calvin and T'oegye agree fully in recognition that the restoration of ontological humanity (*imago Dei* and *T'ien-ming*) requires both external and internal means.

Calvin articulated this in the doctrines of justification and sanctification. In his theology, justification refers to the external imputation of righteousness, and sanctification means the inner process of continual struggle under the direction of the Holy Spirit toward the restoration of the *imago Dei*. T'oegye's teaching of the 'dwelling in the reverence' and the 'investigating the principle' consists in a similar structure. In his confuciology, the investigating the principle refers to an epistemology of knowing the principle, and the dwelling in the reverence implies a practice toward the embodiment of original humanity (*hsing*), i.e., *T'ien-ming*. T'oegye also used other expressions such as the 'investigating the principle and perfecting the nature' and "re-embodying Heaven and progressing along the Way."[75] These expressions also resonate with Calvin's doctrines of justification and sanctification.

T'oegye's doctrine of 'blocking human desires and preserving Heavenly principles' also has a thick resemblance with Calvin's doctrine of sanctification.[76] Calvin's doctrine of sanctification would be described in a comparable way; namely, 'blocking the sinful human desires in the power of the Holy Spirit and preserving the *image Dei* restored by the faith in Jesus Christ.' For Calvin, the whole purpose of sanctification is to restore a lost order through the restoration of image of God in us. In fact, the work of Christ denotes nothing other than this restoration of the original rectitude (*li*) by the regeneration of the image of God in us.

Calvin and T'oegye are same in delineating the corresponding relationship of reverence (*pietas* and *ching*) and righteousness (justice and *i*). On the one hand, Calvin said, "Piety and justice express the two tables of the law; therefore of these two attitudes the wholeness of life is constituted."[77] For Calvin, reverence basically implies our basic relationship to God (the first commandment), while justice (love) does that for our fellow human beings (the second commandment). On the other hand, T'oegye said, "We must make the inside of the mind-and-heart upright by reverence and the outside straight by righteousness," while maintaining both reverence and righteousness.[78] For T'oegye, *ching* refers to the inward disposition (tranquility), and *i* to the outward (activity). Both of them further suggested expanding this just outward relationship to nature (cosmos).

Both Calvin and T'oegye put a special emphasis on dwelling in the reverence (*pietas* and *ching*). Calvin took the doctrine of sanctification as seriously as Karl Barth who called Calvin "a theologian of sanctification."[79] Likewise, T'oegye is called 'a philosopher of *ching*.' Moreover, the teachings of Calvin and T'oegye converge in the common quest of full humanity by the investigation of the original rectitude or principle. Their objects of investigation are radically different, i.e., Jesus Christ (the Word) for Calvin and the Great Ultimate (*li*) for T'oegye. Their expressions for the ground of being (transcendental relationship) are also different, i.e., God (*imago Dei*) and Heaven (*T'ien-ming*). Nevertheless, if these *a priori* dimensions are bracketed, Calvin's doctrine of sanctification entails basically the same mode as T'oegye's teaching of self-cultivation, the dwelling in the reverence and the investigating the principle. As we have discussed already, furthermore, except the idiosyncratic differences between God and Heaven, the teachings of Calvin and T'oegye on original humanity (*imago Dei* and *T'ien-ming*) are strikingly similar and almost mutually interchangeable. Hence, it is not much to say that Calvin's theology and T'oegye's confuciology show striking similarities within their radical differences of their axiomatic presuppositions. Calvin and T'oegye, who lived almost at the same period of history but in two radically different worlds, are extraordinarily comparable partners for dialogue.

4. Ecological Vision of Reverence: *Pietas* Meets *Ching*

Calvin and T'oegye had a similar view on human's relationship with nature. With the doctrines of the image of God and the Heavenly endowment, both of them denied the qualitative differences between humanity and nature. In the narrow definition, only humanity can function as the true mirror of their transcendental ground of being. In the wider definition, nevertheless, humans and things are same as the common image of God and the common Heavenly endowed nature. T'oegye explained their differences in terms of 'physical disposition.' A human being consists of upright and transparent ch'i, *whereas things are composed of leaned and opaque* ch'i. *Hence, the posture of human bodies is upright (toward Heaven), that of wild animals is horizontal (parallel to the Earth), and plants grow vertically in a reverse direction. Calvin also agreed to this point, "God made man erect, unlike the other creatures, that he might know and worship God." Finally, Calvin and T'oegye converge at a similar vision that the transcendent (God and Heaven), the human, and cosmos are closely interrelated (in terms of the* imago Dei *and the* T'ien-ming). *From this vantage point, Calvin and T'oegye seem to agree in advocating a theanthropocosmic (the transcendent, human, and nature interrelated) vision. In this view, human beings are not so much vicious conquers of the universe or the sole independent subjects of history in the linear cosmos, as interdependent co-spectators to witness the glorious cosmic drama of God or ecological keepers to harmonizing the wonderful trajectory of Heaven in the theanthropocosmic theater.*

According to Calvin, there are no "qualitative differences" between human beings and natural things, because they are created in the same image of God. Hence, the wider definition of *imago Dei* includes not only human beings but also natural things. Since all creatures are the works of God, all things in the cosmos, small or large, possess the image of God, a capacity to reflect the glory of God. However, the narrow definition of *imago Dei* comprises only human beings who can perform the true function of creatures like a clear mirror: "While the entire created order reflects God's glory as in a mirror and in this sense 'images' of God, man is distinguished from the mute creation by his ability to reflect God's glory in a conscious response of thankfulness."[80] This is related to the outward physical appearances among creatures. Calvin admitted, "while all other living things being bent over earthward, man has been given a face uplifted, bidden to gaze heavenward and to raise his countenance to the stairs."[81]

God's commandment to humanity for the "dominion over the earth" does not endorse the right of control and domination to abuse and exploit the nature for our own benefits. On the contrary, it implies our obligation to take good care of the cosmos, as a steward of the wonderful garden of God. A person can exercise one's just dominion over the earth, only when "his dominion over the world becomes part of the way in which he as man images the glory of God."[82] Gerrish summarized well:

> Man's being points beyond him to the source of his existence and of the existence of all that is. He was fashioned as the point of creation at which the overflowing goodness of the Creator was to be "mirrored" or reflected back again in thankful reverence. This is the condition from which he fell, no longer the voice of God; and it is the condition to which, through hearing the Word of God in Jesus Christ, he is restored. For all Calvin's persuasion that man has a privileged standing in the world, his cosmos is not man-centered: man has his place as spectator and even agent of the manifestation of God's glory, in which alone the cosmos has its final meaning. It may well be that, when demythologized, such an austere view of the dignity and finitude of man takes no profounder relevance than Calvin ever dreamed of, as Western man moves out of the tight little world of the Middle Ages into the immense, mysterious cosmos of the modern astronomer."[83]

Battles also agreed with this point: "[Calvin] enunciated a principle of Christian stewardship of nature and of style of living that speaks of our present ecological crisis. Before the great technological advances of recent centuries, before the present age of extraterrestrial exploration, Calvin knew the planet Earth was what we today call a 'closed eco-system.'"[84] In the sixteenth century, Calvin already mentioned about 'peace, justice, and preservation of the creation:' "Moreover, that this economy and this diligence, with respect to those good things which God has given us to enjoy, may flourish among us; let every one regard himself as the steward of God in all things which he possess. Then he will neither conduct himself dissolutely, nor corrupt by abuse those things which God requires to be preserved."[85]

T'oegye included not only humanity but also nature and cosmos in his revised *Diagram of* T'ien-ming. He also delineated that humanity and nature are made of the same *T'ien-ming*, an endowment from Heaven. In this Neo-Confucian cosmology, Heaven, humanity, and nature (cosmos) are closely interconnected through the same principle and original nature. But the differences between humanity and nature are not in quality but in function. They are different because they consist in different 'physical dispositions.' Whereas nature is composed of a leaned and opaque physical disposition, Human beings are endowed by an upright and transparent physical disposition. Hence, only human beings possess a capacity of 'knowing and perceiving' and morality.

The *Diagram of* T'ien-ming explains the postural differences among humans, animals, and plants. The posture of human body is square and upright toward Heaven, because human beings possess a transparent and pure physical disposition. That of animals and beasts is horizontal and parallel to the Earth, because their capacity of 'knowing and perceiving' is opened toward only one direction. But plants and trees grow vertically in a reverse direction, because their capacity of 'knowing and perceiving' is completely blocked. Summarizing this in the phraseology of 'humanity and things are same in the nature but different in the material,' Keum put this relationship in the following diagram.[86]

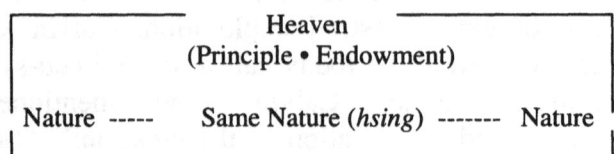

Of course, Calvin did not know the concept of *ch'i* and 'physical disposition.' However, if Heaven were identified with God, the principle and the endowment with Christ and the image, Calvin would have agreed with this diagram. After all, Calvin and T'oegye seem to have a similar vision for the relationships among the transcendent (Heaven or God), humanity, and cosmos. Furthermore, unlike that in Chinese Neo-Confucianism, T'oegye's concept of Heaven includes a personal dimension, as he criticized the doctrine of mechanic correspondence of Heaven and humanity (Tung Chung-shu) but advocated the personal corresponding relationship between Heaven and humanity.[87] This personal corresponding relationship contains the way of faith and reverence for the Lord on High. Pushing one step forward, Keum argued that T'oegye's concept of Heaven involves in a bipolar expression of 'reverence and fear' and 'benevolence and love,' analogous to Rudolf Otto's idea of the holy, *mysterium tremendum et fascinas*.[88] If the interpretations of Lee Sang-eun and Keum Jang-tae are accurate, T'oegye's concept of Heaven would have a notable affinity with the Christian notion of personal God.

The external and internal practices of *ching*, "the single, consistent thread which runs through"[89] the life and thought of T'oegye, points to its climax; that is to say, "Behave as if you were present before the Lord on High." After all, we need not be merely a contingent frame of reference but an absolute ground of being such as Heaven or God in order to maintain the mind-and-heart fully in respect of other people and genuinely in love of myriad things. We must realize the ultimate reality that we are present in front of the Lord on High (cf., *coram Deo*). The Neo-Confucian doctrines of *T'ien-ming*, the endowment from Heaven, and *T'ien-li*, the Heavenly Principle, already disclose this transcendent and ontological ground of original humanity.

At this point also, we find a common thread that connects the whole thoughts of Calvin and T'oegye. We need the ultimate ground of all beings whatever we name it, whether God or the Lord on High. The just and righteous relationship among all beings can be truly realized only when they are based on a proper relationship with this ultimate ground of being. Calvin and T'oegye called this attitude and effort to make the mind-and-heart in this proper relationship reverence (*pietas* or *ching*). We must treat neighbors and nature in reverence and thanksgiving as much as we are facing with God or the Lord on High. Reverence is not only the way toward God but also the way to establish a proper relationship with other people and natural things. Hence, Calvin and T'oegye placed a doctrinal precedence in the concept of reverence. This attitude of reverence gives profound implications to us in today's ecological crisis. Summarizing T'oegye's ecological vision in terms of the reverence of Heaven, the benevolence of people, and the love of things, Keum placed their relations in the following diagram:[90]

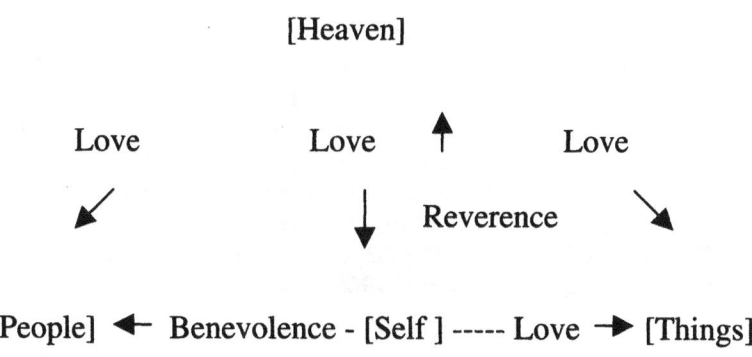

Finally, Calvin's doctrine of *image Dei* (*pietas*) and T'oegye's teaching of *T'ien-ming* (*ching*) converge at a similar vision that the transcendent (God or Heaven), humanity, and cosmos are closely interrelated. Calvin and T'oegye seem to agree in advocating a 'theanthropocosmic' vision. "The Admonition for the Studio of Reverence" which T'oegye included as the ninth in his *Ten Diagrams* exhorts, "Select the ground and tread so carefully to turn around (not to step into) an anthill."[91] From this vantage point, human beings are not so much vicious conquerors of the universe or the sole independent subjects of history in the linear cosmos. But, according to Calvin and T'oegye, they are interdependent co-spectators to witness the glorious cosmic drama of God or ecological keepers to harmonizing the wonderful trajectory of Heaven in this theanthropocosmic theatre.

Notes

[1] The honorific name of Yi Hwang. His courtesy name was Kyŏngho. However, he has been more widely known by T'oegye. For a brief introduction to his life, see Michael C. Kalton, "Introduction," *To Become a Sage: The Ten Diagrams on Sage Learning by Yi T'oegye*, (New York: Columbia University Press, 1988), 14-28.

[2] In fact, Korean people are not unfamiliar with this sort of massive religious structuring. In Chosŏn Dynasty (1392-1910), Neo-Confucianism had permeated to the society in an even more systematic and pervasive way so that it had built Chosŏn culturally and socially as the most confucianized society in the history of East Asia. See Tu Wei-ming, *Confucianism in a Historical Perspective* (Singapore: The Institute of East Asian Philosophies, 1989), 35; and James H. Grayson, "The Study of Korean Religion & Their Role in Inter-Religious Dialogue," *Inculturation* 3:4 (1988): 8.

[3] *Calvin: Institutes of The Christian Religion*, 2 vols., John T. McNeill, ed., Ford Lewis Battles, tr., *The Library of Christian Classics XX and XXI* (Philadelphia: Westminster Press, 1960); abb., *Inst*.

⁴ *Sŏnghak sipdo*. English Translation: Michael C. Kalton, *To Become a Sage: The Ten Diagrams on Sage Learning by Yi T'oegye*; abb., *Diagrams*.

⁵ See Heup Young Kim, *Wang Yang-ming and Karl Barth: A Confucian-Christian Dialogue* (Lanham: University Press of America, 1996), 176.

⁶ Ibid., 138-9.

⁷ Ibid., 175-8.

⁸ Interestingly, T'oegye not only knew but also emphasized to use the comparative method of the 'sameness-in-difference' or the 'difference-in-sameness,' in his famous four-seven debates with Ki Taesŭng. T'oegye said, "Approaching what is unified one must recognize differentiation, and approaching what is differentiated one must see the unity" (*T'oegye chŏnsŏ* [*The Complete Works of T'oegye*]; abb. TGCS] [Seoul: Songgyungwan Taehakkyo, 1985], A, 16.10b). Also, see Sasoon Yun, *Critical Issues in Neo-Confucian Thought: The Philosophy of Yi T'oegye*, tr. by Michael C. Kalton (Seoul: Korea University Press, 1990), 44.

⁹ In the very beginning of the *Institutes*, Calvin stated, "Nearly all the wisdom we possess, that is to say, true and sound wisdom, consists of two parts: the knowledge of God and of ourselves. But, while joined by many bonds, which one precedes and brings forth the other is not easy to discern." (*Inst.* 1.1.1 [35]). See the important book of T. F. Torrance, *Calvin's Doctrine of Man* (London: Lutterworth Press, 1949).

¹⁰ I fully recognize the significance of using inclusive language. For citations in this paper, nevertheless, I will follow the texts as they are.

¹¹ Gerrish, "The Mirror of God's Goodness: A Key Metaphor in Calvin's View of Man," in Donald K. McKim, ed., *Readings in Calvin's Theology* (Grand Rapids: Baker Book House Co., 1984), 108.

¹² Benjamin A. Reist, *A Reading of Calvin's Institutes,* (Louisville: Westminster/John Knox Press, 1991), 9; Gerrish, "Mirror," 108.

¹³ Kalton, *Diagrams*, 23.

¹⁴ Keum Chang-tae, *T'oegyeui sarmgoa cholhak* [The life and Philosophy of T'oegye] (Seoul: Seoul National University Press, 1998), 136.

¹⁵ *Diagrams*, 50.

¹⁶ Chan Wing-tsit, ed. , tr., *A Source Book in Chinese Philosophy* (Princeton: Princeton University Press, 1963), 98.

¹⁷ Keum, *T'oegye*, 130.

¹⁸ See Gerrish's important article: "The Mirror of God's Goodness: A Key Metaphor in Calvin's View of Man," in McKim: 107-122.

¹⁹ Gerrish, "Mirror," 114.

²⁰ See Keum, *T'oegye*, 123, 127.

[21] Calvin, *Comm. on Gen.* 1:26.
[22] *Inst.* 1.15.3 (1:188).
[23] See the third and seventh diagrams (*Diagrams*, 66-9; 143-9); also Keum, *T'oegye*, 131.
[24] *Inst.*, 1.15.4.
[25] *Inst.*, 2.1.5; 3.3.9; 3.18.1; 3.20.42.
[26] Calvin, *Comm. on Gen.* 2:18; 2:21f.; *Inst.* 2.2.13; 2.8.39; 3.7.6.
[27] Calvin, *Comm. on Gen.* 2: 18; *on 1 Cor.* 11:12; also see Torrance, *Man*, 43.
[28] See Kim, *Wang Yang-ming and Karl Barth*, 43-6, 86-90, 158-60
[29] Torrance, *Man*, 77.
[30] Calvin, *Comm. on Gen.* 1: 26.
[31] For T'oegye, self-cultivation as the prime learning of Confucianism can be attained through the Learning of the Way, which is also called Sage Learning.
[32] See an important biography of Calvin, William J. Bousma, *John Calvin: A Sixteenth Century Portrait* (New York, Oxford: Oxford University Press, 1988).
[33] Calvin, *Comm. on Gen.* 1:26.
[34] Gerrish, "Mirror," 108.
[35] See Kalton, "introduction," *Diagrams*, 9-19. In 1550, T'oegye's brother Yi Hae died from the severity of beating.
[36] For the terminology of *t'i-yung* (*ch'e-yong*), see Kalton, *Diagram*, 211-2.
[37] Torrance, *Man*, 19.
[38] Ibid., 20.
[39] Ibid., 83.
[40] Ibid., 101.
[41] Ibid., 105.
[42] Ibid., 106.
[43] Ibid., 116.
[44] See *Inst.* 2.1.8; 3.3.11,12, etc.
[45] Torrance, *Man*, 124, n. 1.
[46] For this view, T'oegye used the Diagram of Ch'eng Lin-yin (1279-1368). See *Diagrams* 6-a.
[47] See *Diagrams* 6-c.
[48] Ch'eng said, "The 'mind of the infant' is the 'naturally good mind' before it has been disturbed by human desires; the 'human mind' is the mind that has been awakened to desire. The 'mind of the great man' is the 'original mind' which is perfectly endowed with moral principle; the 'mind

of the Tao' is the mind that has been awakened to moral principle." Kalton, *Diagrams*, 160.

[49] TGCS. 39. 24.
[50] TGCS. 40. 9.
[51] TGCS. 25, 20.
[52] TGCS. 8. 18.
[53] TGCS. 37. 34.
[54] Ford Lewis Battles, "True Piety According to Calvin," in McKim, *Readings*, 192.
[55] Torrance, *Man*, 86.
[56] Ibid., 128.
[57] Ibid., 128.
[58] *Inst.* 4.14.5; 4.19.7.
[59] *Inst.* 4.14.12; 4.19.7.
[60] Torrance, *Man*, 147 or 145.
[61] Ibid., 129. See *Inst.* 3.7.1.ff.; 3.8.1ff.
[62] See "Christian Life" in *Inst.* 3; also Gerrish, "Mirror," 108.
[63] Lucian Joseph Richard, *The Spirituality of John Calvin* (Atlanta: John Knox Press, 1974), 114; Battles, "Piety," 192.
[64] Richard, *Spirituality*, 114.
[65] Battles, "True Piety," 196.
[66] Ibid., 193.
[67] TGCS. A, 25.25b; tr. cited from Yun, *Issues*, 33.
[68] TGS (*T'oegye jip* [*The Works of T'oegye*]). 41, 27-28.
[69] TGCS. A, 21.25b; cited from Yun Sasoon, *Critical Issues in Neo-Confucian Thought: The Philosophy of Yi T'oegye*, tr. by Michael C. Kalton (Korea University Press, 1990), 30.
[70] *Diagrams*, 87. Kalton translated *ching* (kyŏng) as 'mindfulness.' For an explanation on the term *ching*, see Kalton, "Appendix," *Diagrams*, 212-4. However, I translate it as "reverence" to compare with Calvin's term *pietas*.
[71] *Diagrams*, 162.
[72] T'oegye said that in this state of perfection one can attain the "true news."
[73] *Diagrams*, 169.
[74] *Diagrams*, 36.
[75] *Diagrams*, 144; Keum, *T'oegye*, 141.
[76] DeBary characterized the teaching of 'blocking human desires and preserving Heavenly principle' as a Neo-Confucian moral "rigorism," and differentiated it "from the more exclusively negative focus of western Puritanism" (*Diagrams*, 169; also see Wm. Theodore deBary, *Neo-*

Confucian Orthodoxy and the Learning of the Mind-and-Heart [New York: Columbia University Press, 1981], 67-185). This distinction may be true in a comparison of Neo-Confucianism and Puritanism, but not wholly true in a comparison of Calvin and T'oegye. The bipolar structure of this Neo-Confucian teaching does contain the positive side, whereas Puritanism concerns excessively with sin and evil. However, as we have seen already, the theology of Calvin also consists in a bipolar structure of two inseparable doctrines of justification and sanctification. In fact, this emphasis of sanctification is a point at which Calvin's theology departed radically from Luther's theology.

[77] Calvin, *Comm. Lk.*, 2:25. Cited from Richard, *Spirituality*, 117.

[78] TGS. 36, 15.

[79] Barth, *Church Dogmatics, Vol. IV:2*, tr. G. W. Bromiley (Edinburgh: T.&T. Clark, 1958), 510-1; also Kim, *Wang Yang-ming and Karl Barth*, 76.

[80] Gerrish, "Mirror," 114.

[81] Ovid, *Metamorphoses* I. 84ff.; Calvin cited in 1.15.3.

[82] Torrance, *Man*, 25.

[83] Gerrish, "Mirror," 122.

[84] Battles, "Piety," 203.

[85] John Calvin, *Comm. On Gen.* 2:15, trans. John King, 2 vols. (Edinburgh: Calvin Translation Society, 1847-50), vol. 1, 125; cited from Battles, "Piety," 203.

[86] See Keum, *T'oegye*, 178.

[87] See Lee Sang-Eun, "Life and Scholarship of T'oegye," *Lee Sang-eun sŏnsaeng chŏnjip [The Complete Works of Master Lee Sang-eun: Korean Philosophy]*, Vol. 2 (Seoul: Yemoonseowon, 1998), 135.

[88] See Keum, *T'oegye*, 136. Cf. the diagram of Battles in note.

[89] *Diagrams*, 34.

[90] Keum, *T'oegye*, 184.

[91] Cf. *Diagrams*, 178.

PART II

CHRIST AS THE TAO: EAST ASIAN CONSTRUCTIVE THEOLOGY

Chapter Four

Owning Up To Our Own Metaphors: A Christian Journey in the Confucian Wilderness

1. A Journey in the Confucian Wilderness

In the summer of 1998, I stayed for a month in an art colony in the district of Andong, an ancient city in a southeastern part of Korea. Famous for the preservation of our cultural heritages, particularly Neo-Confucian tradition, this area is recognized as the last stronghold of the Korean culture. (Korea, not China, is the most Confucianized country.)[1] Hidden deep in the mountains, it is free from the noise, disturbances, pollution, and other by-products of the rapid industrialization of this so-called a "tiger" country in the Far East. It is rare to find such a place today that preserves the beauty and solitude of the old Confucian Korea, a country previously recognized as "the hermit kingdom" or "the country of the morning calm" (as the great Indian poet Tagore once called it).

The main mansion in the colony, a typical home of Confucian literati in the 17th century, is composed of three compartments; an inner chamber, an outer chamber, and a shrine hall. This architecture epitomizes the way of living in the traditional Korean society. Women in the inner chamber were engaged in the procreation of descendents, rearing children, and housekeeping. Men in the outer chamber dealt with everyday matters in relation to the outside world. And occasionally all of the family members assembled in the shrine to perform ancestor rites. This arrangement, first of all, signifies a lucid division of labor among the traditional household. Its more profound implication, however, lies in their comprehension of community that is closely related to the notion of time. The inner chamber, as a womb of the house, is assigned to the preparation for the future of the family (descendents), the outer chamber to the present affairs (the living), and the shrine to their communal memory of the past (ancestors). Here, community does not imply merely a temporal gathering of family members presently living together, but includes both those in the past and those yet to come. (Almost every family in Korea preserves a genealogy, a comprehensively written record for the lives of their ancestors from the beginning to the present.) People in this society lived their everyday lives in intimate association with their collective past and future. Community here holds a transhistorical nature.

The transhistorical nature of community reaches its peak in the ancestor rite, a memorial service for those who have passed away. Both the family of the house and the relatives living near and far gather together to participate in the ritual. The participants remember that they share the common collective past, the common memory of the same ancestors. And they experience a transhistorical moment to transcend their separations in space and time to be united again as one community, one collective identity. In addition, sharing food constitutes an important part in this ritual. After dedicating food to their ancestors, they set the table to eat together with guests and their children. There is a certain parallelism between ancestor rites and Christian communion. In the communion, participants also realize their collective identity as a Christian, sharing bread and wine with the common memory of Jesus Christ. Hence, the ancestor rite plays a significant role as a cultural sacrament for this family-centered society.

Spiritually, furthermore, I felt at home in the colony. With a keen interest in Christian spirituality, I had surveyed various Christian retreat centers, ranging from a Pentecostal prayer house to a Benedictine monastery. Although overwhelmed by their fervent prayers and rich traditions, I was not completely sure that I belonged there. In the solitude and carelessness of the Neo-Confucian wilderness, I felt genuine spiritual freedom.

Returning to the spiritual realm that Taoists describe as Nature in non-action action,[2] I could experience deep relaxation and charming delight in being one with God.

Frankly, this experience surprised me. Elsewhere, I have made a confession about my existential struggle as a Christian who has been raised in a Korean family steeped in a thousand-year history in Confucianism: "The more I study Christian theology, the more I become convinced how deeply Confucianism is embedded in my soul and body, my spirituality. Subtly but powerfully, Confucianism still works inside me, as my native religious language. If theology involves the response of one's total being to God, it entails a critical wrestling with this embedded Confucian tradition. Doing East Asian theology necessarily involves the study of Confucianism as a theological task."[3] Although I declared this theologically, spiritually, I had been hesitant to adopt those methods and principles that I learned from our own spiritual traditions such as Confucian quiet sitting, Buddhist Zen meditation, and Taoist breathing technique. As the first Christian convert in the family who acquired a full theological education in the West (America), I was still not free from the educated taboo against non-Christian spiritual practices. However, the experiences in the colony liberated me from the taboo. More deeply than I had realized, our own religions are rooted in my spirituality to constitute an essential part of my spiritual identity (something like a religio-cultural DNA), yet the Western Christianity I was taught superficially hangs about. Spiritually and religiously, Confucianism and Taoism (Neo-Confucianism) still function as my native languages, while the Western Christianity remains as a foreign language like English.

In this context, the Western form of Christianity is not enough, appropriate, or viable. I need a new form of Christianity. To be fully Christian, I should be able to utter my faith and experiences of God in my own native religious languages, as fully--without restraint and shame--as possible. I do need to *own up* to my own religions. In this regard, I completely agree with the statements that Dr. Anto Karokaran, the chief editor of the *Third Millennium*, made in his letter to me: "In this context, it is absolute necessary that church should be able to *own up* the genius, religions, experience, yearnings and the spiritual heritage of people. That alone will give the churches in Asia in-depth identity with the people. If we in Asia really seek an identity of our own church, this can be attained only through an owning up of the religions and traditions of our people. Surely an integration of these with the God-experience in Christ is to be effected."

"Owning up the religions of one's own country as part of one's identity." Yes, but not so much in a pejorative sense (a confession of guilt) as in a constructive sense (a full acknowledgement). Generally, "to own up" means "to admit or confess frankly and fully" (*Webster's Third International Dictionary*). We should be frank and honest about the spiritual, religious, and cultural traditions of our own country to fully confess that they are important parts of our own identity, functioning as native religious languages or spiritual DNA. Any Christian identity disconnected from our own people, community, and collective identity is not only inappropriate but also false. To articulate our Christian identity in the fullest way, I argue that we need to move one step forward. That is to say, we should critically appreciate the symbols and the metaphors of our religions and cultures and apply to our theological thinking, which is the most important meaning of owning up. This does not entail merely a translation of Western Christianity into our religious languages, or a speculative syncretism of multiple religious traditions, but a confession of the integrated Christian selfhood in the network of our own community.

The colony, the last stronghold of Korean culture and spirituality, presented me with profound symbolic implications. There I could find the heart of our Korean spiritual and cultural identity. I cannot complete my mission in doing Korean theology unless I respond properly to those symbols, metaphors, and messages crying out from the depth of our collective soul. I regard them as a barometer or a vantage point to examine the appropriateness of Korea theology. Hence, owning up to our own religions and culture as part of our own identity entails two tasks; 1) critically examining theology from this Korean vantage point and 2) theologically owning up to our own metaphors and symbols. In the remaining discourse, I deal with these two subjects. In the next section, I criticize three prevailing doctrines in Korean theologies; namely, soteriology, the doctrine of original sin, and religious pluralism. In the final section, I suggest a new paradigm of Asian theology by owning up to the Tao (the Way), a religio-cultural root-metaphor for East Asian people; namely, theo-tao (theology as the way of life).

2. Theology from the Korean Vantage Point

1) Soteriology

The Salvation of Jesus Christ is not temporal and partial, but transhistorical and complete. It empowers us to transcend our existential limitation in space and time to be united with the Ultimate Being. If one justifies the sacrifice of the others in the community one comes from for the sake of one's salvation, it is not only a violation of the Gospel of Jesus Christ who taught us sacrificial love on the cross, but also a distortion of Christian soteriology with an ideology of individualism. In order for the Gospel to be truly good news for Asian people, the Christian doctrine of salvation should surmount a soteriological individualism but incorporate the transhistorical nature of the community we discussed. Christian salvation is by no means limited to the present and the future, but it importantly includes the past. The division of the linear time in terms of the past, the present, and the future is not real but artificial and speculative. The genius of Augustine's great book *Confessions* lies in his enlightenment that there is no true salvation without the salvific dealing with one's past (memories) (though his individualistic interpretation unfortunately gave rise to theological individualism). Overcoming this theological individualism,

Asian theology must own up to and make honest confessions of our own collective memories of the past.

A reason why Confucianism is so attractive to the people in this postmodern period is because it does not conceive of a person as an isolated ego (essentialism) but as a center of relatedness in the network of communal relationships (relational view). From the Asian relational viewpoint, one's salvation in separation with one's own community does not make sense at all. Furthermore, Christianity is no longer a minority religion in Korea, but the most powerful one in the society with the membership of more than a quarter of the total population. No more should the Korean Church praise the dissociation from one's own community and traditions as a victory of Christian faith for salvation or a heroic act of Christian evangelism. Such schizophrenic soteriology of amnesia and individualistic evangelism hinders a proper contextualization of Christianity in Korea. The remarkable membership growth of the Korean Church within the short period of two centuries is often cited as a miracle of modern Christian mission. Yet, Christianity has not been rooted firmly in the Korean soil. Christianity is still recognized as a Western religion in Korea, both in society and in academia. There is Christianity in Korea, but no Korean Christianity! There are Christians in Korea, but no Korean Christians! Therefore, it is an urgent task for us to search our new Christian identities to know what it means to be a Korean Christian in the global context of today. We should be honest with our religio-cultural traditions and make confessions of those collective memories. In order to cultivate Korean Christianity, furthermore, we should be humble enough to admit Christianity as a Korean religion, one among multiple Korean religions.

2) The Doctrine of Original Sin

The individualistic soteriology and missiology of amnesia dissociates people from their own past and communities to impede the Koreanization of Christian faith. Moreover, the Protestant doctrine of original sin is often used venomously to demolish the values and ethics of traditional Confucian society. Augustine's doctrine of original sin was primarily intended to solve the problem of theodicy, but rhetorically exaggerated to dispute Pelagius and Manicheans. Protestantism inflated this doctrine to defend their Reformation principle of *sola fide* (faith alone) against medieval Catholicism. To make the situation even worse, Protestant missionaries implanted this doctrine deliberately to exclude indigenous religions and cultures in fear of syncretism. However, religious plurality is an everyday reality for the people in Korea and Asia. For example, in a family, the father is a stern Confucian, the mother a pious Buddhist, the grandmother a customary Shamanist, the son a carefree Taoist, the daughter-in-law a gentle Catholic, the daughter an evangelical Protestant, and the son-in-law a careless atheist. All religions except Christianity have existed in this country more than a millennium. However, we see many cases that the excessive doctrine of original sin plays an ill-fated role in breaking up a previously peaceful familial community. Being self-righteous as a born again Christian, a newly converted Christian daughter accuses indiscriminately the others in her own family--parents, siblings, and spouse--as being "non-Christian" sinners and aggressively teaches them with the "right" doctrines.

The central principle for the Korean society before the advent of Christianity was the Confucian notion of human morality and fiduciary community, based on a Mencian belief in original goodness of humanity. Taking for granted that these relationships are made in accordance to the Heavenly decree, we believed the eternal bond among family and the faithfulness of our friends. In this society, we could fully trust our own family and neighbors, and regarded it as a cardinal virtue to make sacrifices to rectify the name of our family and to keep faithfulness with our friends. Nevertheless, the Christian doctrine of original sin shattered this foundational principle of the Confucian society. Family and friends are no longer 'we," but "they." Since they are also merely sinners, we cannot fully trust them. The doctrine of original sin plays a certain role to bring about the destruction of Confucian society. However, Korean Christianity seems not to have been successful in establishing an alternative societal principle in the moral vacuum made after the withdrawal of Confucianism. Instead, extreme forms of materialism and individualism are rampant. The Confucian belief in fiduciary community and human faithfulness at least enabled us to keep confidence and hope in our own people and society. Unfortunately, however, the Christian doctrine of original sin has helped to foster severe distrust prevailing over the people in the contemporary Korean society.

3) Religious Pluralism

Religious Pluralism is a Western concept that originated from an epistemological shock that Western theologians and scholars from religiously homogenous Christian backgrounds experienced when they encountered and realized the profundities of other religions. Hence, advocates for religious pluralism generally have no real experience in a multi-religious situation that is common to Asian people, an example of which we saw in the Korean family. Religious pluralism legitimately corrects the abuses of eccesiocentric soteriology that sanctions the Church for the exclusive hegemony over salvation and revelation, but still conceals an epistemological immodesty to know everything from the Western center.

Therefore, it is inadequate and odd for us to engage in the Western debates of religious pluralism. For more than a millennium before Christianity came to this land, there already had existed plural religions such as Taoism, Confucianism, Buddhism, and Shamanism. These living traditions have shaped our religious and cultural identities, something like our religious gene or cultural DNA. Those religions are ontologically given to our existences. They are not others but our own. We do not have an epistemological distance to put them in the subject-object dichotomy. An urgent task of Korean theology is not in a speculative discussion of religious pluralism but in an articulation of our Christian identity in this context of religious plurality. Korean religions for us are not so much a subject of religious epistemology as an immediate matter of theological hermeneutics. In proper reverence to our own Korean religions and by owning up to them as part of our own identity, Christian theology should help Christianity take part in the religious plurality of our country.

3. Owning Up To Our Own Metaphors: Towards a Theo-tao[4]

Theologies have developed through continuous paradigm shifts in relation to their surrounding religions and cultures, some times by owning up to their root-metaphors.[5] Generally, theologies can be divided in two paradigms, the logos paradigm and the praxis paradigm. The logos paradigm had been developed by owning up to a key concept of Greek philosophy, logos, as the root-metaphor of theology (theo-logos), and flourished for almost two millennia. However, in addition to its metaphysical and dogmatic propensities, Enlightenment rationalism reduced the logos to a set of technical knowledge. Then, liberation theologies uncovered the sociological plots hidden in the metaphysics of orthodoxy. Instead, they adopted an alternate root-metaphor, praxis, to develop the praxis paradigm (theo-praxis). Although its emancipatory emphasis is historically a necessary corrective, theo-praxis cannot present a comprehensive program without its dialectical counterpart, theo-logy.

Asian theologies seem to inherit this dualism. On the one hand, Asian theologies of the conservative camps uncritically import the Western logos theologies with the blind belief in the myth of orthodoxy. On the other hand, creative Asian theologies, while being reactionary to the logos theology, are not much beyond the corrective manifesto of liberation theology for orthopraxis. The socioeconomic situations of Asia do call Asian theology to adopt the emancipatory tenet of theopraxis. However, the praxis paradigm consists in the modern myth of history, an unqualified belief in teleological progress.[6] Unlike its dualistic, exclusive, and mechanistic Western counterparts, Asian religious visions are more wholistic, inclusive, and ecological. Asian theology as an integrated articulation of the Asian Christian community of faith about God, humanity, and life in the world, should be not only emancipatory, but also open-ended, dialogical, ecological, and inclusive. We should construct a new paradigm of Asian theology that can break down the vicious circle of the socioeconomic injustice prevailing in Asia and at the same time that can own up to Asian religions and cultures as part of our identities.

God cannot be reduced into the logos or the praxis, but God transcends Greek dualism such as form and matter, body and soul, or theory and practice. I argue that the tao (way), a cardinal religio-cultural metaphor of East Asian people, is the root-metaphor, that is more appropriate and Biblical, for Christian theology in coming millennium than the logos and the praxis. The tao is the ultimate way of life, as Jesus said, "I am the way, truth, and life" (Jn 14: 6a). Jesus did not identify himself either as true God (*verus Deus*) and true man (*verus homo*) or as the incarnate logos, but he simply said that he is the Way (Tao) toward God (Jn. 14: 6b). He is Christ in such a way that he was a fully embodied Tao of God. Also remember that the Greek word *hodos* (way) was the original name for Christianity (Act 9:2; 19:9; 22:4; 24:14, 22). I call this tao paradigm *theo-tao* vis-à-vis theo-logy and theo-praxis. Theotao calls forth a theological paradigm shift, from a mechanistic and materialistic paradigm to an organismic and life-generating one. The tao means both the source of cosmic being (logos) and the way of historical becoming (praxis). That is to say the being in becoming, or the logos in transformative praxis. The tao is not an option of either-or, but embraces the whole of both-and. The tao as the ultimate way embodies the transformative praxis of the cosmic trajectory of life in the unity of knowing and acting and with a preferential option toward the sociocosmic biography of the exploited life.

The primary concern of traditional theology is the epistemology of faith, and that of modern theopraxis the eschatology of hope; but the cardinal theme of Asian theotao is the pneumatology of love. Theology is classically defined as the *faith-seeking-understanding (fides quaerens intellectum)*, and theopraxis as the *hope-seeking-practice*; but theotao defines itself as the *love-seeking-way*. Theology (God-talk) focuses on the right understanding of the Christian doctrines (orthodoxy), and theopraxis (God-walk) on the right practice of the Christian ideologies (orthopraxis); theotao (God-live) searches for the wisdom of Christian life (orthotao). What Jesus taught us was not an orthodox doctrine, a philosophical theology, a manual of orthopraxis, or an ideology of social revolution, but the way of life towards God. Jesus Christ cannot be divided between the historical Jesus (theopraxis) and the kerygmatic Christ (theology). Rather, theotao conceives Jesus Christ as the crossroad of the Heavenly Tao and the human tao. It comprehends Jesus as the crucified Tao that reveals the way of salvation, with his own sociocosmic biography of the exploited life. It receives Christ as the Tao of resurrection, the way of sociocosmic reconciliation and sanctification. Jesus Christ teaches us the tao of how we, cosmic sojourners, can live fully human in solidarity with other cosmic co-sojourners. Theotao as a tao of Asian people invites us to participate in the common quest for our true subjectivity, in solidarity with the exploited life including minjung, women, and polluted nature, through the pneumatology of outpouring and harmonizing *ch'i* (spiritual energy).

Notes

[1] Tu Wei-ming, *Confucianism in a Historical Perspective* (Singapore: The Institute of East Asian Philosophies, 1989), 35.

[2] Bede Griffiths, *Universal Wisdom: A Journey Through the Sacred Wisdom of the World* (San Francisco: HarperSanfrancisco, 1994), 27-28.

[3] Heup Young Kim, *Wang Yang-ming and Karl Barth: A Confucian-Christian Dialogue* (Lanham, New York, London: University Press of America, 1996), 1.

[4] For more detailed explanation, see the next chapter.

[5] Hans Küng, *Christianity: Essence, History, and Culture*, tr. John Bowden (New York: The Continuum Publishing Co., 1995).

[6] Raimond Panikkar, *The Cosmotheandric Experience* (Maryknoll: Orbis, 1993).

Chapter Five

God as the Tao:
Toward a Theotao

1. A Call for a Macro-Paradigm Shift in Theology

There is no *the theology*, objective, universal, and relevant to every context. There are *theologies*, open-ended, always on the way, and in dialogue with surrounding cultures and religions. Historically, theologies have developed through continuous paradigm shifts with changes in their relating cultures.[1] Even in the post-modern period, I argue, Western theologies are divided basically in two macro-paradigms--the logos paradigm (theo-logy) and the praxis paradigm (theo-praxis)--both holding leftovers of the Greek dualism (form and matter, soul and body, theory and practice, etc.).

1) The Logos Paradigm
Traditional Western theologies developed in dialogue with Greek philosophy and flourished for almost two millennia since the employment of the key concept of the latter, logos, as the root-metaphor of theology (theos + logos). In the early Christian Church, *theologia* had wider meanings, interrelated with *sophia* (wisdom) and others.[2] However, the narrower definitions of later Christian theologians, for instances, of logos as logical and technical knowledge, and the excessive focus of Protestant theologians on the Word of God made this paradigm more and more metaphysical, dogmatic, and phonocentric. The goal of theology, primarily as God-talk, is to transmit the universal orthodoxy. However, most contemporary theologians claim that this logosphonocentric paradigm is anachronistic and is no longer viable, not to mention criticisms from deconstructionists such as J. Derrida.

2) The Praxis Paradigm

Since Latin American liberation theologies uncovered the sociological plots in the metaphysics of orthodoxy, the logos paradigm has been under fire. Various liberationist theologies and first world political theologies argue for the employment of a somewhat neglected root-metaphor, praxis. In the praxis paradigm, theology (precisely, theopraxis) is defined rather as God-walk, and orthopraxis becomes the primary issue instead of orthodoxy. The emancipatory emphasis of Christian practice is the necessary and legitimate corrective to the traditional theology. However, the praxis paradigm can hardly present an independent and comprehensive program, because it is incomplete without the logos and still remains within the boundary of the Western dualism between theory and practice. Both the logos and praxis paradigms hold to this hierarchical Western dualism and, hence, are basically heteronomous, whatever distinctions they make between super-structure and infrastructure or between heteronomy and autonomy. A subtler problem in the praxis paradigm is its uncritical belief in the dialectical progress of history. The strength of theopraxis is its expression of the emancipatory dimension, but it is weak in facilitating the ecological and dialogical dimensions, highly demanded in our broken, polluted, postmodern world.

Yet, most Asian theologies seem to remain within the boundaries of these dualistic macro-paradigms. On the one hand, Asian theologies of the conservative camps uncritically import the western logos theologies with the blind belief in the myth of orthodoxy. On the other hand, creative Asian theologies, while being reactionary to the logos theology, are not much beyond the corrective manifesto of liberation theology for orthopraxis. The socioeconomic situations of Asia do call Asian theology to adapt the emancipatory tenet of theopraxis. However, Asian theology needs to admit that the hidden presupposition of the praxis paradigm consists in the modern myth of history, a belief in teleological progress, whose validity is now questionable.[3]

Furthermore, non-linear Asian religious visions challenge Asian theologians to demythologize this myth of history, the modern modification of salvation history inherited from Judeo-Christianity. Unlike its dualistic and mechanistic Western counterparts, Asian religious visions are characteristically more holistic, inclusive, and ecological; namely, "anthropocosmic" (humanity and cosmos being interrelated) or even "theanthropocosmic" (God, humanity, and cosmos being interrelated).⁴ Eventually, these visions will provide rich resources for Asian theology. Asian theology in the 21st century, as an integrated articulation of the Asian Christian community of faith about God, humanity, and life in the world at a given time, should be not only emancipatory, but also open-ended, dialogical, ecological, inclusive, and holistic. However, Asian theology of religions, active in inter- and intra-religious dialogue, has been too politically naïve and too retrospectively romantic. A most important issue for Asian theologians today is how to construct an Asian revolutionary theology to break the vicious circle of the socioeconomic injustice prevailing in Asia without falling into Western dualism and historicism.⁵

3) The Tao Paradigm

Constructing such a viable Asian theology for the 21st century solicits a macro-paradigm shift beyond the two paradigms of the traditional logos-oriented theo-logy and the modern praxis-oriented theo-praxis. The days for these two Western root-metaphors for theology, logos and praxis, have passed. Asian theology in the day of new wine needs a new wineskin. I argue that the East Asian root-metaphor of tao is the new wineskin (though it is also as old as logos and praxis in the history of East Asian thought, but, perhaps, new for Christianity).⁶

Then, what is Tao? First and foremost, just as God is, tao is inexplicable. You would be idolatrous if you define it with any intention. Compare "The Tao that can be told of is not the eternal Tao" (*Tao-te Ching*) and "You shall not make yourself an idol, whether in the form of anything that is in heaven above, on the beneath, or in the water under the earth" (Ex. 20: 4). In light of the biblical expression of Jesus, we might say provisionally that Tao is the ultimate way of life, as Jesus said, "I am the way, truth, and life" (Jn 14: 6a). In fact, Jesus did not identify himself as either *verus Deus* and *verus homo* or the incarnate logos, but he simply said that he is the Tao toward God (Jn. 14: 6b). He is Christ in such a way that he was a fully embodied Tao of God. In that sense, Jesus was *the* way to God (Jn. 14: 6b), without reference to any so-called exclusivism.

2. The Ugŭmch'i Phenomenon

What does the tao paradigm look like? Kim Chi Ha, a well-known Korean poet, once told an intriguing story in his essay, "The Ugŭmch'i Phenomenon."[7] This story suggests an example of the tao paradigm. It introduces some valuable insights helping us to envision a theology in the East Asian way of life and to solve the problematic of Asian theology, an inner conflict between the Christian liberation imperative and Asian anthropocosmic vision. I will begin with this story to search a new tao paradigm of Christian theology.

1) The Ugŭmch'i Phenomenon

In front of my house in Haenam,[8] there is a little stream. This stream originates from Kumgang-bo, the largest reservoir in the neighborhood of Haenam. In the past, the water was so clean and fresh that people could swim and catch fish in the stream. Now, however, it has become a smelling ditch, darkly rotten with waste water, synthetic detergents, briquette ashes, garbage, Coke bottles, cans, etc. Nevertheless, the stream changes into an entirely different shape when it rains. At midnight, it makes a sound as big as what we can hear from refreshing rapids in Mt. Sŏlak or Mt. Odae. And it sweeps off wastes downward so that it becomes as clean again as it used to be. When I sat down by the stream and noticed it had much better fishes jumping, I was greatly astonished. There are about ten big cement stepping-stones across the stream, and rapid currents flow down between them like a waterfall. This scene forms a little spectacle. Alas, there are many fishes jumping from below to cross over the stepping-stones in order to return upward! It is a great scene with scores of fishes in various sizes from little daces to hand-sized crucians continuously jumping up and straining.

I sat down by the stream and thought over and over.

How on earth can those fishes move upward against such strong downward currents? Is it only what evolution theory calls a groping in the dark which leads to endless failure? To see that some among them go upward very smoothly, it seems not to be a failure or a groping in the dark. What on earth is the mystery that enables them to do so? Unless those fishes are fools, there is no reason why they so persistently put forth every ounce of their energies in vain. It must be obvious to them that they swim upward in the opposition to the currents pouring down upon them. But I do not know more. Perhaps, the fishes are returning to the reservoir to find the ecological conditions most appropriate to them in terms of water temperature, water pressure, water *habitus*, plankton, etc. However, how can they swim upward along the water currents flooding downward so rapidly and forcefully? It might be enough to explain that it is a mysterious creation of the Creator. But this still does not solve the mystery. It is easy and simple to say that it is an adaptation to the environment according to evolutionary theory. But that does not explain everything, either.

In the night, I sat down with crossed legs and looked at the face of my wife, straight at the pupils of her eyes. At that time, a strange thought occurred to me. Through her eye-pupils, I could feel what she was thinking in her mind, and, through my pupils, my wife likewise felt that I could feel the same. It happened for an instant. It was like the movement of spirit or vital spirit or vital energy (*sin-ki*).⁹ I realized then that it is the movement of *sin-ki* insofar as one movement of *sin-ki* enables to know the other movement of *sin-ki* and vice versa.

Aha, now I know.

The mystery of how a feeble fish can swim upward along the turbulent down flow to return to its destined birthplace.
That is to say, such a thing occurs in the moment when the *sin-ki* of a fish is united with the *sin-ki* of the water flow. Nature is another good word for this. In other words, it happens in the moment when the nature of a fish is united with the nature of water.

The *ch'i* (*ki*)¹⁰ of water moves in both directions of *yin* and *yang*.¹¹ While the *yang* of water runs the downward movement, the *yin* of water runs the upward movement. While water flows downward, water flows upward at the same time. In the river, there must occur counter-currents in the majestic movement of big waters! This is a phenomenon that occurs simultaneously in the movement of *il-ki* of water.¹² This phenomenon arises exactly when the nature of a fish's *sin-ki* becomes united with the nature of this *ch'i*. Does history progress forward only? No. While history progresses forward, it goes backward at the same time. Although it is described in terms of quality and quantity, this is a matter that arises simultaneously. Certainly, it is not right to say this in terms of either front and back or progression and retrogression. Rather, it would be better to say this in terms of a simultaneously converging-diverging movement of 'in and out' and 'quality and quantity'. And all the movements after all return to their origin. They return, not in vain but creatively. This is the *yin-yang* movement of *il-ki*, i.e., the primordial vigor of the cosmos. Humans can do this with self-consciousness.

Aha, I also know now.

From the palpitation of the persistent and dynamic *sin-ki* of the fishes in returning home, [I now understand] the mystery of the Ugŭmch'i War¹³ where the exulted *sin-ki* had the minjung¹⁴ of several hundred thousands jumping soaked with blood and going persistently upstream.

We should not understand it simply as a battle or a struggle in terms of victory or failure between this and that. By that understanding, we fail to see or, after all, misconceive the mystery of that tremendous collective life energy discharged by the minjung in the Tonghak Revolution in 1894. It may end with such misconceptions as a literary expression like the explosion of continuously accumulated *han*[15] or as a superficial socio-economic observation like an upward uprising or a poverty uprising.

But it is not.

Although it looks like that, it is not.

Han, poverty, or the demand for class liberation, without the knowledge of the movement of minjung's collective *sin-ki* that acts in everything, cannot uncover the mystery of Ugŭmch'i. Nor can *han*, poverty, or the demand for class liberation receive a legitimate evaluation on the basis of historical meaning.

What kind of force, on the earth, did make the minjung of several hundred thousands who were almost bare handed, though armed only with firelocks and bamboo spears, attempt to climb the hill through the scorching fires of the demonic cannons of Japan and the Yi Dynasty?[16] What was the origin of the power that empowered them to advance for freedom, forming a mountain of corpses and a sea of blood, experiencing failure after failure, and crossing death over death?

Where is the clue to understand the mystery of Tonghak that had constituted incessantly the roots of the main forces in the righteous armies of 1895, in the second and the third great righteous armies, and in the Minhoe Movement during the Russo-Japanese War, again in the March First Movement, in the Ch'ŭngudang Movement[17] of the Ch'ŭndogyo, in many tenancy disputes in the peasant history of Chosŭn,[18] in strike movements in the labor history of Chosŭn, in the movements of numberless liberation armies in Kando, Siberia, Tumen River, and in the region of Yalu River, and in the movements of the underground organizations to support them, and going further even in the change of the forms of ideologies and organizations?

In short, it is in the great self-awakening of minjung on the collective *sin-ki* through Tonghak. Minjung became aware of and is the embodiment of vitalization and spiritualization and the vital energy *ch'i* that endlessly and immensely evolves, socializes, self-sanctifies, and self-divinizes.

The collective *sin-ki* of the self-conscious minjung is a great cosmic movement to be united with the primordial *sin-ki* of history, i.e., the *yin-yang* movement of *ch'i*, against the demonic currents of the history that poured down against them. I will call this the ugŭmch'i phenomenon.

Ah, Ah. The *sin-ki* of our minjung, the vitalization and spiritualization, with the climax of 1894, has been displaced, alienated, rooted out, oppressed, disgraced, divided, imprisoned, neglected, destroyed, and enslaved—therefore, has been slaughtered until now--by the wrong foreign ideas of the West or Japan. Even now, the flags of death are waving in the street. Only few people are searching around for the true subjectivity of minjung.

This is the time when we look into the ugŭmch'i phenomenon in order to find our genuine subjectivity.

Yes. For, even against the demonic currents of the history, we have not failed completely and descended out, but have ascended this much!

3. The Phenomenology of *Sin-ki (Shen-ch'i)*

This provocative story of the ugŭmch'i phenomenon puzzles the dualistically oriented western mind in general and the analytically trained modern mind in particular (including the westernized Asian mind). However, it is a very original East Asian way of grasping reality, and it is theologically profound. Furthermore, it includes some passwords that open the vision of a new East Asian paradigm in theology. Although it requires further thematization, it would be worthwhile mentioning five points at this juncture.

1) Neither the logos nor the praxis paradigms fit simply with this phenomenology of *sin-ki* and fall short of the analogical imaginations which it presents. If the polluted flood metaphorically refers to the force of destruction, the feeble fishes represent the force of life. Deconstuctionists have unveiled that the logosphonocentric paradigm has had more affinity to the force of destruction than the force of life. It rather has helped the demonic movement of the historical flood, by its involvement with sociological plots such as androcentricism and ethnocentricism, and by endangering life by its dualistic fragmentation.

Although the praxis paradigm aggressively resists the force of destruction, it remains within the limit of narrowly defined historico-socio-economic concerns that do not proceed completely beyond the logic which the force of destruction constitutes. It does not propound a self-sufficient description for the force of life, but ends with a reactionary articulation against the force of destruction. Nor does it retain a profound understanding of the complex relation among God, humanity, and the cosmos such as those expressed in the Asian theanthropocosmic vision and the phenomenology of *sin-ki*.

2) The ugŭmch'i phenomenon lures Asian theology one step forward. For example, Korean minjung theologies have made some valuable contributions to contemporary theology with the prophetic calling to the Christian movement for justice and freedom in solidarity with minjung. Yet, this call seems to be too narrow, romantic, or Western to grasp fully the Asian profundity, from the perspective of Kim Chi Ha's ugŭmch'i phenomenon.

Kim Yong-bock argued that the social biography (the

underside history) of minjung is a more authentic historical point of reference for theological reflection than the doctrinal discourses (the official history) superimposed by the Church and in the orientation of Western rationality.[19] It was an important creative proposal for Asian theology to be situated on a concrete ground so as to evoke the self-awakening of minjung as the subjects of history. To employ the sociobiography of minjung as a main theological agenda serves as a legitimate correction to traditional theology, primarily based on autobiographical (psychological) or church (official) narratives. Nevertheless, this more or less exclusive focus upon the political economy of God looks too historical to be liberated fully from the myth of history in Western modernism and to locate Asian religious dimensions properly.

Chung Hyun Kyung's provocative proposal of *"hanpuri"* (a participatory event to release *han*-riddenness) was an authentic appeal from the perspective of Korean women.[20] Asian theology should take seriously the reality of *han*, the accumulated psychosomatic experiences (and dangerous memory) of collective suffering. The *hanpuri* does have psychologically and socially therapeutic and salvific dimensions. Nevertheless, with such a simple hermeneutics of *han*, we cannot reach the depth of Asian spiritual complexity, as Kim Chi Ha claimed in the ŭmch'i phenomenon. To thematize Christian confessional agendas more comprehensively in the profundity of Asian spiritual complexity, Asian theology needs to move forward beyond the proposals of these minjung theologies so as to overcome this potential reductionism (or "misconceptions," according to Kim Chi Ha).

3) **The Hermeneutics of *Ch'i***: Kim Chi Ha's phenomenology of *sin-ki*, though based on his creative interpretation of the original Tonghak, offers some fascinating clues for the re-visioning of Asian theology for the 21st century beyond the (Western) logos paradigm and the (Asian) praxis

paradigm. It illuminates that *ch'i*, a term very comparable to *pneuma*, renders a significant hermeneutical key and rich theological resources for Asian theologies in the future. He argues lucidly that *ch'i* (more correctly, *sin-ki*) is the key to unveil the reason for the mystery of how the feeble fishes in the turbulent flood and the multitude of minjung in the Ugŭmch'i War can manifest such a tremendously life-empowering force. *Ch'i* is a very East Asian term, like *pneuma*, not dualistic and analytic, but holistic and embracing, while it is both the source (primordial energy) and the medium of primordial empowerment. Hence, with this new hermeneutics of *sin-ki*, we can develop an appropriate answer to our starting question; how to construct a revolutionary theology to fight against the vicious structure of socio-economic injustice without falling into dualism and historicism. An answer would be a revolutionary theology of *sin-ki* with the hermeneutics of *ch'i*.

4) **The Pneumatoanthropocosmic Vision**: The phenomenology of *sin-ki* expands the East Asian anthropocosmic vision to the new horizon in the unity of Heaven (God), the human, and Earth (cosmos) through the spirit (*ch'i*). Neo-Confucianism developed a vision of 'cosmic togetherness' in an organismic unity with Heaven, Earth, and the myriad things, as well expressed in Chang Tsai's *Western Inscription*:

> Heaven is my father and Earth is my mother, and even such a small creature as I find an intimate place in their midst. Therefore that which fills the universe I regard as my body and that which directs the universe I consider as my nature. All people are my brothers and sisters, and all things are my companions.[21]

Kim Chi Ha enhanced this East Asian anthropocosmic vision dramatically by the phenomenology of *sin-ki*. Since it implies a spiritual communion between humanity and the universe through the interpenetration of *ch'i*, I call it pneumatoanthropocosmic vision. In East Asian thought, this vision is heavily embedded in the *yin-yang* correlation, the sophisticated cosmology of Changes (*I-Ching*), the Neo-Confucian metaphysics of the Great Ultimate (*T'ai-chi*), etc. The anthropocosmic vision expressed in various Asian religions should be a reservoir of great potential to heal, vitalize, and even save today's fragile and fragmented Christian theologies from the swamp of postmodern crises, as many Asian and Western scholars suggest.

Nevertheless, this potentiality does not necessarily endorse a retrospective and uncritical romanticization of Asian religions and cultures. On the contrary, it should be emphasized that Asian religious visions are not totally innocent in the genealogy of distortion and exploitation. Historically, they also committed much evil against minjung and women. For example, Cheng Chung-ying succinctly characterized the East Asian mode of orientation in terms of "natural naturalization" (nature and naturality in Chinese philosophy: *I Ching/Tao Te Ching*) and "human immanentization" (Confucianism and Neo-Confucianism), which contrasts with the Western mode in terms of "rational rationalization" (reason and rationality in Greek philosophy: Socrates/Plato/Aristotle) and "divine transcendentalization" (Judeo-Christianity).[22] Although this is a lucid distinction, we must question whether such a beautiful mode of natural naturalization and human immanentization does not contain the dimension for a paradise indwelling, the myth that has been broken. (A big question is why those who inherit those beautiful ecological traditions now live in the most polluted regions in the world?) The human reality people experience today is rather in a post-paradise situation. Christianity is at least correct in that observation. After the lost battle vis-à-vis Western modernization, we Asians can no longer be "innocent dreamers" (Paul Tillich). We need to employ modern critical thinking and a hermeneutics of suspicion. At the same time, we must admit with the postmodern consciousness that the modern mode of thinking has reached its limits and that there might be hope in our own resources, though they must be reinterpreted in new ways.

From this vantage point, the revolutionary theology of *sin-ki* should take very seriously Asian hermeneutics of suspicion including minjung, feminism, neo- and post-colonialism, and orientalism. Asian theology in the future solicits an entirely new paradigm that can utilize fully the profundity of the Asian pneumatoanthropocosmic vision, while remaining faithful to these Asian hermeneutics of suspicion.

5) The Sociocosmic Narrative of the Exploited Life: By reinforcing Kim Yong-bock's proposal with the pneumatoanthropocosmic vision, we could commence the thematization of an Asian revolutionary theology of *sin-ki*. In addition to the sociobiography of minjung, Asian theology should embrace also the cosmic biography of the exploited life (metaphorically, the feeble fishes in the turbulent currents). Asian theology should liberate the underside of history of the exploited life including animals and nature from the captivity of modern imperialism and scientific fundamentalism that could bring us the doomsday of massive ecological destruction. As hinted in the ugŭmch'i phenomenon, the Asian pneumatoanthropocosmic vision cultivates a symbiosis of the life network through the communication of *ch'i*. This vision fosters the human race's relationship with other lives more holistically and profoundly than *societas* (by contract), *communitas* (by fellowship [*koinonia*]). While being enhanced by a holistic vision, Asian theology should demythologize the dimensions of innocent dreaming and individualistic mysticism in the Asian anthropocosmic visions. To do it, Asian theology needs to thematize what I call the *sociocosmic narrative of the exploited life*, creatively pushing beyond both the sociobiography of minjung and the anthropocosmic vision. Asian theologians are impelled to tell the story of the sociocosmic network of the exploited life constituted by the spiritual communion of *ch'i* whose primordial energy is salvific, both emancipatory and reconciliatory. The ugŭmch'i phenomenon is an example of such a sociocosmic narrative of the exploited life, metaphorically telling the story of the two exploited lives, the feeble fishes in the turbulent stream and the multitude of minjung in the Ugŭmch'i War.

4. A Tao of Asian Theology in the 21st Century

God can be reduced neither to logos nor to praxis. God cannot be fully grasped with these two dualistic root-metaphors. God transcends Greek dualisms such as form and matter, body and soul, divinity and humanity, logos and praxis. I have argued that the tao is a root-metaphor to articulate God more appropriately than these two metaphors. I call this theological paradigm to be constructed with the root-metaphor of tao *theotao* (theos + tao) vis-à-vis theology (theos + logos) and theopraxis (theos + praxis).

In the light of the ugŭmch'i phenomenon, theotao, as a proper Asian theology in the 21st century, envisions the Tao of God operative in the pneumatoanthropocosmic trajectory. Theotao introduces an Asian pneumatological hermeneutics of *ch'i* that embodies the vital energy in exploited lives so as for them to swim dynamically upward against the demonic down-flood of history, e.g., the manipulative global market controlled by technocratic dictatorship and centralized cyber space in our days. To do that, theotao calls forth Asian theology to make a macro-paradigm shift from the mechanistic cosmology to that of life, from the materialistic paradigm to that of *ch'i*, and ontological paradigm to that of life-generating.

As its Chinese word consists of two ideographs, meaning 'head' (*t'i*, being) and 'vehicle' (*yung*, becoming), tao means both the source of being (logos) and the way of cosmic becoming (praxis). Accordingly, tao can be reduced neither to being nor to becoming; rather it is the being in becoming or the logos in transformative praxis. Tao is not an option of either-or, but embraces the whole of both-and. It does not force one to stay at the crossroad of logos (being) and praxis (becoming), but actualizes one to participate in a dynamic movement to be united with the cosmic track.[23] The tao as the ultimate way and reality embodies the transformative praxis of the sociocosmic trajectory of life in the unity of knowing and acting. Hence, while theology is the perspective from above and while theopraxis that from below, theotao is the perspective from an entirely different dimension, theanthropocosmic intersubjectivity, or in the light of the ugŭmch'i phenomenon, pneumatoanthropocosmic communion (through the network of *ch'i*). Furthermore, as already mentioned, it particularly focuses on the sociocosmic biography of the exploited life.

Theotao argues that Asian theology can be neither logos-centric (knowledge) nor praxis-centric (acting), but tao-centric (*sophia* in action). Asian theology as a theotao can be reduced neither to an orthodoxy (a right doctrine of the church) nor to an othopraxis (a right practice in history), but should embrace holistically the right way of life (orthotao), the transformative wisdom of living in a pneumatoanthropocosmic trajectory. The issue is neither only an orthodoxy nor only an orthopraxis, but an orthotao, i.e., whether we are in the right way of God revealed in Jesus Christ and live wisely under the direction of the Holy Spirit. Remember that the Greek word *hodos* (the Way, also meaning path, road, route, journey, march, etc.) was the original name for Christianity (Act 9:2; 19:9; 22:4; 24:14, 22). Hence, the key issue is whether we are in proper communication with the Spirit to participate fully in the loving process of theanthropocosmic reconciliation and sanctification. See the end of 1 Corinthian 13! If orthodoxy emphasizes faith and if orthopraxis hope, the orthotao focuses on love. Whereas the primary theme of the traditional logos theology was the epistemology of faith and whereas that of the modern praxis theology was the eschatology of hope, the cardinal theme of Asian tao theology is the pneumatology of love (that is the goal of the hermeneutics of *ch'i*). A comparison between the following two Christian and Taoist statements illuminates the gravity of this pneumatology of love:

> Love never ends. But as for prophecies [theopraxis], they will come to an end; as for tongues, they will cease; as for knowledge [theology], it will come to end. For we know only in part, and we prophesy only in part; but when the complete comes, the partial will come to an end. When I was a child, I spoke like a child, I thought like a child, I reasoned like a child; when I became an adult, I put an end to childish ways. For now we see in a mirror dimly, but then we will see face to face. Now I know only in part; then I will know fully; even as I have been fully known. And now faith, hope, and love abide, these three; and the greatest of these is love. (1 Cor. 13:8-13).

> The fish trap exists because of the fish; once you've gotten the fish, you can forget the trap. The rabbit snare exists because of the rabbit; once you've gotten the rabbit, you can forget the snare. Words exist because of meaning; once you've gotten the meaning, you can forget the words. Where can I find a man [sic] who has forgotten words so that I can have a word with him [sic]? (Chuang Tzu)[24]

Asian theology as a theotao takes the definition of the *love-seeking-tao* rather than the classical definition of theology, the *faith-seeking-understanding* (*fides quaerens intellectum* [theology]), or the *hope-seeking-practice* (theopraxis). Whereas theology (God-talk) focuses on the right understanding of the Christian doctrines and whereas theopraxis (God-walk) the right practice of the Christian ideologies, theotao (God-live) searches for the way and wisdom of Christian life. In fact, Jesus taught neither an orthodox doctrine, a philosophical theology, a manual of orthopraxis, nor an ideology of social revolution, but the tao of life and living. Jesus Christ cannot be divided between the historical Jesus (theopraxis) and the kerygmatic Christ (theology). Hence, with the first Korean Catholic theologian Yi Pyŭk (1754-1786),[25] theotao conceives Jesus as the crossroad of the Heavenly Tao and the human tao; that is to say, the pneumatoanthropocosmic Tao. Further, theotao comprehends Jesus as the crucified Tao that reveals the way of salvation, with his own sociocosmic biography of the exploited life. Furthermore, theotao sees Jesus as the Tao of resurrection, the way of cosmic reconciliation and sanctification that teaches us how we, cosmic sojourners, can live fully human in solidarity with other cosmic co-sojourners, particularly with the fullness of other exploited lives.

Finally, the tao of Asian theology in the 21st century is to invite us to participate in the common quest for the true subjectivity of the exploited life including minjung, women, and polluted nature through the hermeneutics of *ch'i*. In light of the ugŭmch'i phenomenon, the tao of Asian theology revitalizes us by the outpouring power of the *sin-ki* (*ch'i*) through self-awakening. That has been manifested in the sociocosmic narratives of the exploited lives in Asia, but "has been displaced, alienated, rooted out, oppressed, disgraced, divided, imprisoned, neglected, destroyed, and enslaved— therefore, has been slaughtered until now--by the wrong foreign ideas." To re-vision us with the correction of those wrong foreign ideas and re-embody us in the outpouring power of *ch'i* through self-awakening is an important task of theotao, as a new paradigm of Asian theology in the 21st century.

Notes

[1] According to Hans Küng, there are six macro-paradigms in the development of Christianity; Early Christian apocalyptic paradigm, Early Church Hellenistic paradigm, Mediaeval Roman Catholic paradigm, Reformation Protestant paradigm, Enlightenment modern paradigm, contemporary ecumenical paradigm (postmodern). See Küng, tr. by John Bowden, *Christianity: Essence, History, and Culture* (New York: The Continuum Publishing Co., 1995)

[2] See Jean Pepin, "logos," in *The Encyclopedia of Religion*, Vol. 9, ed. by Mircia Eliade (New York: Macmillan Publishing Co., 1987), 9-15; also Edward Farley, *Theologia: The Fragmentation and Unity of Theological*

Education (Philadelphia: Fortress Press, 1983), 31-44, 162, 165-169.

³ On this point, we need to listen carefully to Raimond Panikkar's analysis; see his *The Cosmotheandric Experience* (Maryknoll: Orbis, 1993).

⁴ For the anthropocosmic vision, see Tu Wei-ming, *Centrality and Commonality: An Essay on Confucian Religiousness*, rv. ed. (Albany, NY: State University of New York Press, 1989), 102-107. For the theanthropocosmic vision, see Panikkar. For a comparative study of these, see Heup Young Kim, *Wang Yang-ming and Karl Barth: A Confucian-Christian Dialogue* (Durham: University of Press of America, 1996), 175-177, 185-188.

⁵ Among Asian theologians of the first generation, this dichotomy appeared saliently between Raimond Panikkar and M. M. Thomas; cf. Panikkar, *The Unknown Christ of Hinduism*, rv. ed. (Maryknoll: Orbis, 1964) and Thomas, *The Acknowledged Christ of the Indian Renaissance* (London: SCM Press, 1969). Aloysius Pieris formulated this issue in slightly different way; according to Paul Knitter, "a non dualistic understanding/experience of the liberative activity of God and the liberative activity of the poor as 'one indivisible Saving Reality,'" in his *Asian theology of liberation* (Maryknoll: Orbis, 1988), xiv.

⁶ As the widely used root-metaphor of all classical East Asian religions including Confucianism, Taoism, and Buddhism, tao is a very inclusive term with various meanings. Tentatively, I use the Confucian definition formulated by Herbert Fingarette: "Tao is a Way, a path, a road, and by common metaphorical extension it becomes in ancient China the right Way of life, the Way of governing, the ideal Way of human existence, the Way of the Cosmos, the generative-normative Way (Pattern, path, course) of existence as such" (*Confucius—The Secular as Sacred* [Harper & Row, 1972], 19).

⁷ In *Saengmyŭng* [Life] (Seoul: Sol, 1992), 188-192. Since this essay is theologically profound and worthwhile introducing among Asian theologians, I translate the whole essay here with the permission of the author. Although Kim Chi Ha changed his name to Kim Hyŭng recently, I will use his old name in this paper, because he has been better known by Kim Chi Ha.

⁸ Translator: A city located in Chŭllanamdo, located the Southwestern part of Korea.

⁹ Translator: The Chinese character *shen* (in Korean, *sin*) has various meanings such as ghost, spirit, soul, vitality, sacred, etc. Although this word is translated as vitality in this paper, it includes a connotation of divinity. And *shen-ch'i* is translated as vital energy, but this paper uses primarily its Korean romanization, *sin-ki*, because of its special meaning.

¹⁰ Translator: The Korean romanization of this word *ch'i* is *ki*. *Ch'i* is

very similar to *pneuma* and translated variously such as energy, vital force, material force, and breath. When this word alone is used, this paper takes *ch'i* instead of *ki*, translating as energy.

[11] Translator: *Ch'i* is interpreted to have two forms of movement, the *yin* (negative or female) and the *yang* (positive or male) that forms a unity of complementary opposites such as *T'ai-chi*.

[12] Translator: *Il-ki* (in Chinese, *i-ch'i*) means the one or primordial *ch'i* or the primordial vigor.

[13] It was the last and fiercest battle during the second uprising of Tonghak minjung, which broke out on a hill of Kongju, named Ugŭm, in the December of 1894. (Translator: Tonghak, literary meaning Eastern Learning, was a religious movement founded by Ch'oe Che-u [1824-1864] in reaction to the so called Western Learning, i.e., Catholicism.)

[14] Translator: Minjung literally means the multitude of people, but in minjung theology this term is closely related to the oppressed, exploited, and marginalized groups.

[15] Translator: This term became well known by the use of Korean minjung theologians. According to Suh Nam-dong, *han* is "the suppressed, amassed and condensed experience of oppression caused by mischief or misfortune so that it forms a kind of 'lump' in one's spirit" ("Towards a Theology of Han," *Minjung Theology* [Singapore: CCA, 1981], 65). In fact, Suh's theology of *han* was heavily influenced by Kim Chi Ha's thought. However, afterwards, Kim changed his mind on this issue and went beyond it, as appears in this paper.

[16] Translator: Yi Dynasty is the last dynasty in Korea (1392-1910).

[17] Ch'ŭngudang was a national movement organization of Ch'ŭndogyo organized in North Korea with the institute of religious affairs of Ch'ŭndogyo in North Chosŭn after the independence of August 15, 1945. It attempted a revival movement of the March First Movement in 1948 to develop a general election for the unification of the South and the North. However, the plan was revealed beforehand, many people were arrested, and the movement was systematically suppressed since then.

[18] Translator: Chosŭn is the original name of the Korea.

[19] See Kim, "Theology and the Social Biography of Minjung," *CTC Bulletin* 5:3-6:1 (1984-5), 66-78.

[20] See Chung, "'Han-pu-ri': Doing Theology from Korean Women's Perspective," *The Ecumenical Reviews* 40:1 (Jan, 1988), 27-36.

[21] Chan Wing-tsit, tr., *A Source Book in Chinese Philosophy* (Princeton, N.J.: Princeton University Press, 1963), 497-8. Wang Yang-ming further developed the doctrine of the Oneness of All Things, as expressed in the following. For more discussion, see Heup Young Kim, 42-46:

"The great man regards Heaven, Earth, and the myriad things as one body.

He regards the world as one family and the country as one person. As to those who make a cleavage between objects and distinguish between the self and others, they are small men. That the great man can regard Heaven, Earth, and the myriad things as one body is not because he deliberately wants to do so, but because it is natural humane nature of his mind that he does so. Forming one body with Heaven, Earth, and the myriad things is not only true of the great man. Even the mind of the small man is no different. Only he himself makes it small. Therefore, when he sees a child about to fall into a well, he cannot help a feeling of alarm and commiseration. This shows that his humanity [jen] forms one body with the child. It may be objected that the child belongs to the same species. Again, when he observes the pitiful cries and frightened appearance of birds and animals about to be slaughtered, he cannot help feeling an "inability to bear" their suffering. This shows that his humanity forms one body with birds and animals. It may be objected that birds and animals are sentient beings as he is. But when he sees plants broken and destroyed, he cannot help a feeling of pity. This shows that his humanity forms one body with plants. It may be said that plants are living things as he is. Yet, even when he sees tiles and stones shattered and crushed, he cannot help a feeling of regret. This shows that his humanity forms one body with tiles and stones. This means that even the mind of the small man necessarily has the humanity that forms one body with all. Such a mind is rooted in his Heaven-endowed nature, and is naturally intelligent, clear, and not beclouded." (Chan Wing-tsit, tr., *Instructions for Practical Living and Other Neo-Confucian Writings* [New York: Columbia University Press, 1963], 272)

[22] Cheng Chung-ying, *New Dimension of Confucian and Neo-Confucian Philosophy* (Albany, NY: State University of New York Press, 1991), 4-22.

[23] Tu Wei-ming said: "Since the Way is not known as a norm that establishes a fixed pattern of behavior, a person cannot measure the success or the failure of his conduct in terms of the degree of approximation to an external ideal. The Way is always near at hand, and the journey must be constantly renewed here and now... It is like the art of archery... The Way, then, does not provide an ideal norm or a set of directives to be compiled with. It functions as a governing perspective and a point of orientation." (Tu, *Humanity and Self-cultivation* [Berkeley: Asian Humanities Press, 1979], 36f.; also see 35f.).

[24] Translation from Burton Watson, tr., *The Complete Works Of Chuang Tzu* (New York & London: Columbia University Press, 1968), 302.

[25] See Jean Sang Ri, *Confucius et Jesus Christ: La Premiere Theologie Chrestienne en Coree D'apres L'oeuvre de Yl Piek lettre Confuceen 1754-1786* (Paris: Editions Beauchesne, 1979).

Chapter Six

Jesus Christ as the Tao: Toward a Christotao

> Love never ends. But as for prophecies [praxis], they will come to an end; as for tongues, they will cease; as for knowledge [logos], it will come to end. For we know only in part, and we prophesy only in part; but when the complete comes, the partial will come to an end. When I was a child, I spoke like a child, I thought like a child, I reasoned like a child; when I became an adult, I put an end to childish ways. For now we see in a mirror, dimly, but then we will see face to face. Now I know only in part; then I will know fully; even as I have been fully known. And now faith [logos], hope [praxis], and love [tao] abide, these three; and the greatest of these is love. (St. Paul, 1 Cor. 13:8-13 NRSV)

> The fish trap exists because of the fish; once you've gotten the fish, you can forget the trap. The rabbit snare exists because of the rabbit; once you've gotten the rabbit, you can forget the snare. Words [logos] exist because of meaning; once you've gotten the meaning, you can forget the words. Where can I find a man [of the Tao] who has forgotten words so that I can have a word with him? (*Chuang-tzu*:26).[1]

1. A *Koan*: Christological Impasse

The contemporary christological crisis consists of two basic problems: modern historicism and the dualism in Western thought between logos and praxis. The most salient example of modern historicism in the biblical field is the quest for the historical Jesus that began in the nineteenth century and continues today through the so-called second and third quests.[2] Demanding historical proofs, these scholars have challenged Christian faith and created a strange dichotomy between the historical Jesus and the kerygmatic Christ, between the earthly Jesus and the risen Christ, or between the pre-Easter Jesus and the post-Easter Christ. They reflect a historical positivism or absolutism, an uncritical attitude toward, or a blind faith in the modern myth of history.[3]

The dualism between logos and praxis, two 'root-metaphors' of theology, has deepened with the emergence of liberation theology.[4] Many liberation theologies have radically questioned the relevance of church doctrines to historical situations (esp., in the problem of radical evil). They argue that the primary task of theology has to do with right practice (orthopraxis) to transform unjust socioeconomic conditions, and they reject traditional logos theology (orthodoxy) as an oppressively dogmatic, metaphysically abstract, and naively ahistorical. This powerful challenge divides contemporary systematic theology into two major camps, theo-logy and theo-praxis.[5] This division is further sharpened in christology; namely between christo-logy (Christ as [the incarnate] logos) and christo-praxis (Jesus as the praxis [of the reign of God]).[6]

Despite their holistic religious contexts, Asian theologies are also divided into two poles between Asian liberation theologies (liberationists) and Asian theologies of religions (inculturationists). Focusing on the historical situations of Asia, the liberationists call for an emancipatory struggle for socioeconomic justice; the inculturationists emphasize the contextual and hermeneutical imperative of Asian 'anthropocosmic' (humanity and the cosmos being interrelated) religious visions.[7] A classic example of this dualism appears in the christologies of two great Indian theologians, M. M. Thomas and Raymundo Panikkar.[8] On the one hand, Thomas' *a posteriori* christology sees the functional Christ in the historical and inner transformation (reformation through modernization) of Asia and Asian religions (*The Acknowledged Christ of the Indian Renaissance*). On the other hand, Panikkar's *a priori* christology finds the suprahistorical presence of a homologous Christ in Asian religions (*The Unknown Christ of Hinduism*). In Korean christologies, also, there appears a sharp distinction between the two opposite camps of minjung theology (Jesus as the oppressed people) and contextual theology of religions (Christ as the Sage or Bodhisattva).⁹

Hence, dualism is a dilemma prevalent in contemporary christology. It is an unavoidable consequence as long as a christology holds logos as the root-metaphor, because logos, based on dualistic Greek thinking, is vulnerable to an unfortunate split between theory (logos) and practice (praxis), between form and content, or between thought and feeling. Furthermore, blind faith in the modern myth of scientific history forces Western christologies to reach an impasse, as is soberly illustrated by the recent North American debates among scholars surrounding the Jesus Seminar.¹⁰

How can we get out of this swamp of the dualism between logos and praxis and the myth of history? This is the *koan* (an evocative question) of this paper. That is to say in our context, how can we construct an East Asian christology that neither neglects historical situations nor falls into Western dualism and historicism? In other words, how we can thematize an emancipatory christology embodied in the soteriological nucleus of Asian anthropocosmic religions?

This christological enterprise may call for an entirely new hermeneutical paradigm with a new root-metaphor. I will argue that *tao* is such an alternative root-metaphor for Jesus Christ.¹¹ And I will propose a *christotao* that may overcome the dualism between christology and christopraxis.¹² Vindications for this adoption are already apparent from several sources. First of all, from the confessional point of view, the adoption of tao for the formation of East Asian christology is as legitimate as that of logos was for the fourth-century Christian church in developing the Nicene-Chalcedonian christology. Further, remember that the original title for both Jesus and Christianity was the way (*hodos*) (John 14:6; Acts 16:17, 18:25, 18:26).¹³ Furthermore, contemporary theologies and biblical scholarship illuminate, more and more transparently, the viability and cogency of the adoption of tao as an alternative post-modern title and metaphor for Jesus.

Ironically, the third quest for the historical Jesus seems to have arrived at a conclusion close to my thesis; that is, Jesus is more like a sapiential teacher of the Way (tao), a Sage, than either a founder of orthodox religion (logos) or an eschatological revolutionary (praxis).[14] Western theologian Jürgen Moltmann rejected the classical logos christology and explicitly employed the way-metaphor in his recent christological formulation. He claims, "I am trying to think of Christ no longer statically, as one person in two natures or as a historical personality. I am trying to grasp him dynamically, in the forward movement of God's history with the world." Moreover, Moltmann submits three reasons for the adoption of the way-symbol; it "embodies the aspect of process," "makes us aware that every human christology is historically conditioned and limited," and "invites" the unity of christology and christopraxis.[15]

Asian theologian Aloysius Pieris has also made a helpful suggestion. He has attempted to overcome the division among Asian theologies between liberationists and inculturationists by formulating an Asian liberation theology of religions through a genuine intrareligious dialogue between Asian religions (*Love Meets Wisdom*).[16] In his recent book, he divided Christian theology into three patterns--the logos model ("philosophical or scholastic theology"), the *dabhar* model ("liberation theology"), and the *hodos* model ("theology as search for wholeness"), and searched for a holistic model that "weaves together all three aspects of Christian discourse: Jesus as the *word* that interprets reality, the *medium* that transforms history, and the *way* that leads to the cessation of all discourse."[17]

These are some examples of clear signs anticipating the coming of christotao, the tao paradigm of christology. However, the holistic, but fundamentally apophatic and elusive universe of tao is strange and foreign to modern people (including modernized Asians). We may need an enlightenment to leap into this new hermeneutical vista from the contemporary linear, scientific worldview. This enlightenment requires an experience more profound than that of "rhythmic pulses" and "cosmic dance of energy" which Fritjof Capra described.[18] For an innocent dance of the cosmos is a romantic interpretation of tao. An adequate interpretation must be more complex, because tao is a fully loaded term as old as logos. And tao has often been used in ideologies of the powerful to oppress the powerless in the political history of East Asia. Tao also should be regarded as a broken symbol in a fragmented form. Thus its interpretation must be not only creative and imaginative but also critical. An imaginative hermeneutics of retrieval should be combined with a proper hermeneutics of suspicion.

Kim Chi Ha, a well-known Korean poet, whose thought and practice motivated Korean Christians to formulate minjung theology (a Korean indigenous liberation theology from the perspective of the oppressed people) wrote an insightful essay in which, I think, he made such a critical but imaginative interpretation of tao.[19] I will use this essay "The Ugŭmch'i Phenomenon" as a parable to provoke readers to leap into the world of tao so that we may find a solution to the *koan* of this paper.[20]

2. A Parable: Return of Fish

Summary of the Ugŭmch'i Phenomenon

To heal his sickness from the long period of imprisonment by the military dictatorship, Kim Chi Ha retired to a small city in the southwestern part of Korea. In front of his house there was a little stream. Wastes resulting from regional industrialization now hopelessly polluted the stream, which had been famous for its clean water. Nevertheless, when it rained, the situation changed. The rain not only swept out the wastes but also made the water clean again. Moreover, he was surprised to see many small fish swimming upstream against the flood of water! How could such a feeble fish swim upward against such a turbulent flow? This question puzzled him.

During his meditation with his wife, however, he experienced a transcendental feeling in which his mind became unified with hers so that they were able to read each other's thoughts instantaneously without verbal communication. Suddenly, with this experience, he was enlightened to the fact that such a thing can happen by the work of *sin-ki*[*shen-ch'i*] "vital energy."[21] The movement of one's *sin-ki* capacitates one to know of the *sin-ki* of others. When the *sin-ki* of a feeble fish becomes united with the *sin-ki* of water, it can swim against even a mighty turbulent flood. Furthermore, as *ki*[*ch'i*], "energy," always consists of *yin* and *yang*, the *ki* of water also moves in both directions of *yin* and *yang*. From the exuberant palpitation of the *sin-ki* of many fishes in union with the *yin* movement of the water, Chi Ha discovered a clue to understanding the mystery of the Ugŭmch'i War[22] in which the feeble minjung--literally a multitude of people (in this case several hundred thousands)--fought vigorously against the allied forces of their government and Japanese troops who were armed with powerful mechanized weapons. The collective *sin-ki* inspired and empowered the minjung to participate courageously in the movement and to be united with the primordial *ki*, in the same manner as the feeble fishes which swim vigorously upstream against the formidable flood to be in union with the *yin* movement of water. The fierce palpitation of the minjung against the turbulent flood of historical demons is in fact a great cosmic movement united with the *yin-yang* movement of *ki*. Chi Ha called this the ugŭmch'i phenomenon.

The first realization of Chi Ha in this parable was an ecological insight that nature ("rain") has a self-saving power to bring forth life even in a fateful environment ("the polluted water") seemingly beyond remedy. He saw a hope for life in this spiritually fragmented and ecologically destructive world spawned by the developmental ideology of modern technocized, commercialized, and cemented culture. A more important realization for us, however, is that from the tao world he found the clue to transcending historical dualism and the real source of the life energy which outpours such a vigorous vitality to the feeble fishes and the minjung in Ugŭmch'i.

This marked a radical turning point for his thought. Before this point, Chi Ha was the one who formulated the most creative and subversive Korean hermeneutics of suspicion from the perspective of *han*, "the suppressed, amassed and condensed experience of oppression caused by mischief or misfortune so that it forms a kind of 'lump' in one's spirit."²³ Chi Ha's conception of *han* is comparable to J. B. Metz's notion of "the dangerous memory of collective suffering," though the former refers more closely to a psychosomatic feeling.²⁴ In a manner similar to Metz's formulation of the dangerous memory, Chi Ha argued for a dialectical praxis of *han* in which the minjung use the historically accumulated *han* as the source of transformative energy. He contended that minjung must be awakened to cut themselves from the vicious circle of *han*-riddenness and participate in the emancipatory movement to resolve their *han*. This inspired some progressive Korean theologians to formulate minjung theology, and *han* has become not only a major issue of minjung theology but also a famous idiom in Asian liberation theologies. Some minjung theologians argued even that a main task of theologians is to become a priest of *han* in order to motivate and participate in a movement of *hanpuri* (a collective action to release *han*) of minjung and women.²⁵ After the enlightenment, however, Chi Ha states:

> Aha, I too know now. From the palpitation of the persistent and dynamic *sin-ki* of the fishes in returning home, [I now understand] the mystery of the Ugŭmch'i War where the exultant *sin-ki* had the minjung of several hundred thousands jumping soaked with blood and going persistently upstream. . . . It may end with such misconceptions as a literary expression like the explosion of continuously accumulated *han* or as a superficial socio-economic observation like an upward uprising or a poverty uprising. . . . Although it looks like that, it is not. *Han*, poverty, or the demand for class liberation, without the knowledge of the movement of minjung's collective *sin-ki* that acts in everything,

cannot uncover the mystery of Ugŭmch'i. . . . What kind of force on the earth made the minjung of several hundred thousands, who were almost bare handed, armed only with firelocks and bamboo spears, attempt to climb the hill through the scorching fires of the demonic cannons of Japan and the Yi Dynasty?[26] What was the origin of the power that enabled them to advance for freedom, forming a mountain of corpses and a sea of blood, experiencing failure after failure, and crossing death over death? . . .

The collective *sin-ki* of the self-conscious minjung is a great cosmic movement to be united with the primordial *sin-ki* of history, i.e., the *yin-yang* movement of *ki*, against the demonic currents of the history which poured down against them. I will call this the ugŭmch'i phenomenon. Ah, Ah. The *sin-ki* of our minjung . . . has been displaced, alienated, rooted out, oppressed, disgraced, divided, imprisoned, neglected, destroyed, and enslaved by--therefore, has been slaughtered until now--the wrong foreign ideas of the West or Japan. Even now, the flags of death are waving in the street. Only few people are searching around for the true subjectivity of minjung. This is the time when we look into the ugŭmch'i phenomenon in order to find our genuine subjectivity.

This passage depicts the moment when Chi Ha finally returned to the old tao world and began to formulate a critical and creative hermeneutics of retrieval in and through the tao tradition. It tells of a paradigm shift in his thought from a Korean version of the dualistic mode of contradiction (*han*) to the East Asian correlative mode of complementary opposites (*yin-yang*). The shift involves his enlightenment to the true source of the tremendously life-empowering force manifested by the feeble fishes in the turbulent flood and the multitude of minjung in the Ugŭmch'i War. The key to revealing this mystery of the ugŭmch'i phenomenon is the notion of *ki*, a very East Asian term. Just like *pneuma*, *ki* is not so much dualistic and analytic as holistic and embracing; at the same time, it is both the source (primordial energy) and the medium of primordial empowerment. In the light of this phenomenology of *ki*, the East Asian anthropocosmic vision can be expanded to the new horizon in the unity of Heaven (God), the human, and Earth (cosmos) through the spirit (*ki, pneuma*), namely, "a pneumatoanthropocosmic vision."[27]

Further, this shift involves a hermeneutical leap in his thought, from a linear-historical horizon to the cosmogonic-anthropocosmic horizon of tao. Here is a new Taoist interpretation of history articulated by Chi Ha:

> The *ki* of water moves in both directions of *yin* and *yang*. While the *yang* of water runs the downward movement, the *yin* of water runs the upward movement. While water flows downward, water flows upward at the same time. In the river, there must occur counter-currents in the majestic movement of big waters! This is a phenomenon that occurs simultaneously in the movement of *il-ki* (*i-ch'i*, a primordial energy) of water. This phenomenon arises exactly when the nature of a fish's *sin-ki* becomes united with the nature of this *ki*.
> Does history progress forward only? No. History progresses forward; at the same time, it goes backward. Although it is stated as a matter of quality and quantity, this is a matter that arises simultaneously. . . . [It] is not right to say this in terms of either front and back or progression and retrogression. Rather, it would be better to say this in terms of a simultaneously converging-diverging movement of 'in and out' and 'quality and quantity'. And the whole movement after all returns to its origin. It returns, not in vain but creatively. This is the *yin-yang* movement of *il-ki*, i.e., a primordial *ki* of the cosmos. Humans can do this with self-consciousness.

Furthermore, this tao universe consisting in the cosmogonic rhythm of *yin-yang* compels us to make a paradigm shift in our basic mode of thinking; namely, from the "either-or" thinking of contradiction to the "both-and" thinking of complementarity. In this hermeneutical universe, this is grasped as *T'aegŭk* (the Great Ultimate) or *I* (the Change) through the correlative movement of *yin* and *yang*. Chou Tun-i (1017-1073) summarized the cosmogony in *An Explanation of the Diagram of the Great Ultimate*:

> The Ultimate of Non-being [Non-Ultimate] and also the Great Ultimate! The Great Ultimate through movement generates *yang*. When its activity reaches its limit, it becomes tranquil. Through tranquility the Great Ultimate generates *yin*. When tranquility reaches its limit, activity begins again. So movement and tranquility alternate and become the root of each other, giving rise

to the distinction of *yin* and *yang*, and the two modes are thus established.[28]

3. Tao: A New Root-Metaphor For Jesus Christ

As Jaroslav Pelikan has pointed out, the "momentous" adoption of logos as the title for Jesus (christo-logy) by the fourth-century Christian Church was accompanied by another kind of monumental adaptation of Jesus as the cosmic Christ (the Savior of the cosmos).[29] Although it brought unfortunate consequences in the modern period, the adoption of logos was to articulate not only the cosmic but also the cosmogonic natures of Christ in the Greek philosophical language. The Nicene Creed explicitly states, "We believe in one Lord Jesus Christ, the Son of God . . . through him, all things were made." This faith in the cosmogonic Christ was not new, but had been already articulated by John and Paul: "All things were created through him and for him. He is before all things, and in him all things hold together" (Col. 1:16-7; cf. Jn. 1:3).

Tao is a metaphor more congenial to the cosmogonic nature of Christ than logos: "Tao is Great in all things, complete in all, universal in all, whole in all. These three aspects are distinct, but the reality is one" (*Chuang-tzu*: 22).[30] Tao refers to the ultimate reality beyond the realm of naming with any cultural-linguistic metaphor, symbol, and form; it is radically apophatic: "The Tao that can be told of is not the eternal Tao; The name that can be named is not the eternal name. The Nameless is the origin of Heaven and Earth; The Named is the mother of all things" (*Tao-te ching*: 1).[31] Hence, the naming of tao is only heuristic: "I do not know its name; I call it Tao, for the lack of the better word" (*Tao-te ching*: 25). Remember again that Jesus and primitive Christianity originally had a similar heuristic name, *hodos*.

Tao-te ching describes tao with basically feminine metaphors: "mother of all things," "the root," "the ground" (of Being), or "the uncarved block" (the original nature). Tao is called "the mystical female": "The spirit of the valley never dies. It is called the mystical female. The gateway of the mystical female is called the root of Heaven and Earth" (6). "Can you play the role of the female in the opening and closing the gates of the Heaven?" (10).[32] This feminine vision is based on *Lao-tzu*'s principle of "reversal." A. C. Graham explicated that *Lao-tzu* always put the preferential option to the strategy of *yin* rather than that of *yang* in the following chain of oppositions:[33]

Yang	*Yin*	*Yang*	*Yin*
Something	Nothing	Before	Behind
Doing Something	Doing Nothing	Moving	Still
Knowledge	Ignorance	Big	Small
Male	Female	Strong	Weak
Full	Empty	Hard	Soft
Above	Below	Straight	Bent

This principle of reversal is closely connected with the principle of return. In fact, this is the hidden source for the vitality depicted metaphorically by the return of fish in the ugŭmch'i phenomenon. "Attain complete vacuity, maintain steadfast quietude. All things come into being, and I see thereby their return. All things flourish, but each one returns to its destiny. To return to destiny is called the eternal (Tao). To know the eternal is called enlightenment" (*Tao-te ching* : 16).[34] The paradoxical power of weakness and emptiness is further developed in the principle of *wu-wei* (non-action action). Bede Griffiths (1907-93), a Benedictine mystic who had lived many years in Indian ashrams, made helpful remarks on the implications of *Tao-te ching* to Western religion:

> The most typical concept in the *Tao Te Ching* is that of *wu wei*, that is "actionless activity." It is a state of passivity, of "non-action", but a passivity that is totally active, in the sense of receptivity. This is the essence of the feminine. The woman is made to be passive in relation to the man, to receive the seed which makes her fertile. But this passivity is an active passivity, a receptivity which is dynamic and creative, from which all life

and fruitfulness, all live and communion grow. The world today needs to recover this sense of feminine power, which is complementary to the masculine and without which man becomes dominating, sterile and destructive. But this means that western religion must come to recognize the feminine aspect of God. This leads to *the paradox of the value of emptiness*. "We make pots of clay," it is said, "but it is the empty space in them which makes them useful. We make a wheel with many spokes joined in a hub, but it is the empty space in the hub which makes the wheel go round. We make houses of brick and wood, but it is the empty spaces in the doors and windows that make them habitable." This again is the value of "non-action", what Gandhi called *ahimsa*.[35]

4. Korean Quests for Christotao

How can we conceive Jesus Christ with this new root-metaphor? In fact, Korean Christians in this hermeneutical universe have comprehended Christ from this vantage point of tao since the beginning. For Korean Christians, the adoption of tao as the root-metaphor in understanding Christ is no less legitimate but more congenial than that of logos was for the fourth-century Greco-Roman Christians. The following are three examples of christotao formulated by Korean Christian thinkers, Yi Pyŏk, Ryu Young-mo, and Lee Jung Young.

Jesus as the Crossroads of the Heavenly Tao and the human tao

Lao-tzu claimed that the ultimate Tao (the Way) is apophatic and ineffable beyond human reason and language. At the same time, however, he said even more about sapiential taos (ways) of life (*te*). Tao refers to the heuristic metaphor not only for the ineffable ultimate but also for practical ways people can participate in the transformative praxis of the anthropocosmic trajectory. In the history of East Asian thought, this distinction is normally recognized by the complementary opposites of Taoism and Confucianism.[36] Taoist tradition takes more seriously the apophatic dimension of the Ultimate (the Heavenly Way); Confucian tradition focuses on the kataphatic side of human living (the human way). Hence, Yi Pyŏk (1754-86), the brightest Neo-Confucian scholar of his time, the first Christian theologian in Korea, and the spiritual founder of the Korean Catholic Church, found the unity of these two taos in Jesus Christ.[37] Yi conceived Christ as the Sage *par excellence*, the crossroads of the Heavenly Way and the human way, in whom divinity and humanity become united.[38]

Jesus as Being-in-Non-Being

Ryu Young-mo (1890-1981), a Korean Christian-Taoist ascetic, heavily influenced by Confucianism and Buddhism, thematized the cosmogonic Christ from the deepest heart of the East Asian hermeneutical universe of tao. The statement on the Non-Ultimate and the Great Ultimate in the Chou Tun-i's diagram denotes the ultimate complementary and paradoxical opposites of the ineffable Vacuity and the Cosmogony. From the vantage point of this supreme cosmogonic paradox of Tao, Ryu "understood the cross as both the Non-Ultimate and the Great Ultimate . . . Jesus is the one who manifested the ultimate in Asian cosmology. Through the sacrifice of himself, he achieved genuine humanity (*jen*). That is to say, by offering himself as a sacrifice, he saved the human race and opened the kingdom of God for humanity."[39]

In Christ, the Non-Ultimate and the Great Ultimate become one. In the historical scene, this is revealed as the affectionate and filial relation between father and son, as Jesus uttered, "I [the Son] am in the Father and the Father is in me" (Jn. 14:11). Ryu described the cross as "the blood of the flower" (*kkotpi*)[40] through which the Son reveals the glory of the Father and the Father the glory of the Son. Seeing the blossom of this flower of Jesus (at the cross), he envisioned the glorious blossom of the cosmos (cosmogony). For Ryu, "the cross is a rush into the cosmic trajectory, resurrection is a participation in the revolution of the cosmic trajectory, and lighting up the world is the judgment sitting in the right-hand side of God."[41]

From the perspective of the supreme paradox of non-being and being, Ryu formulated furthermore a unique Korean pneumato-apophatic christotao. He called Jesus "the Primordial Breathing (*sumnim*)." Jesus is the One who "Is" in spite of "Is-Not," that is to say, "Being-in-Non-Being (*Ŏpshi-gyeshin nim*)." Whereas we are those of non-being-in-being, He is the One of Being-in-Non-Being. Whereas we are the "forms" that are "none other than emptiness" (*Heart Sutra*), He is the "emptiness" that is "none other than form."[42]

Jesus as the Perfect Realization of Change

Lee Jung Yong (1935-95), a Korean constructive theologian, formulated an East Asian christology in a systematic fashion with the metaphysics of the Change. Advocating for change as an appropriate mode of future theology, Lee argued consistently for a paradigm shift in the theological mode of thinking from the substantial mode (being), through the process (becoming), to that of change (being and becoming).[43] As the discoveries of modern physics such as Einstein's relativity theory and quantum theory have revealed, the ultimate reality is neither so much being (substance) in Greek metaphysics (Aristotelian logic, Euclidean geometry, and Newtonian physics), nor becoming in (Whiteheadian) process metaphysics, as being and becoming in the Change (or the Great Ultimate in the complementary opposites of *yin* and *yang*). "Change is, then, the matrix of all that was, is, and shall be. It is the ground of all being and becoming. Thus theology of change, which characterizes the ultimate as both being and becoming."[44]

The "either-or" logic is so deeply rooted in the intellectual life of the West that it is hard for Western theology (including process theology) to transcend it. However, the either-or logic is false as Wilfred Smith also said: "In all ultimate matters, truth lies not in an either-or, but in a both-and."[45] Lee argued, the "both-and" logic of change is the right metaphysics of theology (God as the Change). "Change in the *I-Ching* is certainly beyond categorization. It is simultaneously personal and impersonal, male and female, immanent and transcendent."[46] This total affirmation (both-and), however, is complementary to the total negation (neither-nor). In the supreme paradox, the Great Ultimate signifies the total affirmation; the Non-Ultimate the total negation. Hence, God as the great Tao is simultaneously personal and impersonal, male and female, immanent and transcendent; at the same time, however, it is neither personal nor impersonal, neither male nor female, neither immanent nor transcendent.

Furthermore, Jesus Christ can be conceived as the perfect realization of Change:

> In Jesus as the Christ man and God are in perfect harmony. Jesus' identity does not preclude his humanity but presupposes it, just as *yang* presupposes the existence of *yin*. Furthermore, perfect humanity presupposes perfect divinity. In his perfect complementarity of divinity and humanity, or of the change and the changing, he is both perfect man and perfect God. Being the symbol of perfect harmony between the change and the changing, Jesus Christ is the ultimate reality of change and transformation.[47]

Christ as the perfect realization of Change is also both personal and impersonal, male and female, and individual and communal.[48]

Lee's proposal, though it has many brilliant points, has not been paid as much attention as it deserves. His proposal is, perhaps, metaphysically positivistic and excessively rhetorical, as if making a universal claim for change as an alternative metaphysics for a new theology. His hermeneutics of retrieval is excellent, but innocent and romantic, without a proper hermeneutics of suspicion upon his own tradition. His theology is a good model for Asian speculative theology of religions; but not for Asian liberation theology, another pole of Asian theology, without a sufficient consideration of historical situations. In a passionate polemic against the Western metaphysics of contradiction, Lee, contrary to his intention, also fell into the metaphysical assumption that tao can be named objectively. However, tao by definition cannot be described objectively but only heuristically. Tao as the constant change has no fixed face; it has many faces constantly changing from context to context and from people to people. Hence, in the dynamic hermeneutics of tao, the context and the role of an interpreter are mutually important. Tao hermeneutics is a creative and holistic engagement consisting of an interpreter (a community of interpretation), the context, and the trajectory of tao. At the same time, it itself is a tao (skill) for an interpreter to discern how she or he can participate appropriately in the cosmic movement of tao at any given time.

5. Jesus Christ as the Theanthropocosmic[49] TAO

A more profound dimension of tao thinking lies in the possibility of christological utterance with respect to the ultimate in such a way that the ineffable tao can be somehow articulated while transcending fallacies of metaphysical positivism; namely, by the both-and and the neither-nor mode of thinking. In fact, the genius of the Nicene-Chalcedonian formulas lies in its articulation of the ultimate and cosmogonic nature of Christ beyond the Greek dualistic framework. Christian faith empowered the fourth-century Christians to transcend the either-or logic of Greek philosophy. The Nicene Creed (325) used the both-and mode to articulate Christ as both *vere deus* and *vere homo*. Furthermore, the Chalcedonian formula (451) employed the neither-nor mode to express that the two natures in the Christ are neither confused, changed, divided, nor separated. To say it more sharply in East Asian terms, the fourth-century Christians intuitively had perceived the cosmogonic nature of Christ as the supreme paradox of the Great Ultimate (total affirmation of the both-and) and the Non-Ultimate (total negation of the neither-nor).

In fact, this tao mode of paradoxical thought appears not only in the Gnostic Gospels but also in creative early Christian theologians such as Gregory of Nyssa (ca. 395) and Dionysius the Areopagite (fl. 500), in Christian mystics such as Francis of Assisi (1182-1226), Meister Eckhart (d. 1327), and Julian of Norwich (b. 1343), and most explicitly in the principle of *coincidentia oppositorum* formulated by Nicholas of Cusa (1401-64).[50] Remember that St. Paul already proclaimed,

"There is no longer Jew or Greek, there is no longer slave or free, there is no longer male or female...in Christ" (Gal. 3:28).

Christ as the New *T'aegŭk*

With Ryu's profound pneumato-apophatic insights, christotao can be further thematized. Jesus is the Tao, the supreme paradox of the Great Ultimate and the Non-Ultimate (*T'aegŭk* and *Mugŭk*), the Primordial Breathing, the Being-in-Non-Being, and the complete emptiness (*kenosis* or *sunyata*) that is none other than the complete form. The cross refers to the rush to the cosmic path, and resurrection signifies the christological transformation of the *theanthropocosmic* trajectory. The crucifixion of Jesus was a cosmogonic crucifixion which changed the cosmic path. Furthermore, it signifies a radical opening of the vicious circle of the old metaphysical world of Tao (*T'aegŭk* and *I*).[51] This is the great openness of the Ultimate. The cosmogony of the old *T'aegŭk* was crucified into the *Mugŭk*, and resurrected as the New *T'aegŭk*, i.e., a great eschatological movement of the supreme paradox. It is neither just a dogmatic revolution (logos) nor only a messianically inspired social revolution (praxis), but it is a cosmogonic revolution (tao). The christotao of the crucified and risen *T'aegŭk* entails the cosmogonic revolution of the Christ. Christ rushed into the old anthropocosmic cycle of *T'aegŭk* through the crucifixion, changed it to the new "serendipitous" theanthropocomsic trajectory (Tao), and opened the new aeon of *T'aegŭk*.[52]

Christ as the Serendipitous Pneumatosociocosmic Trajectory

This new serendipitous theanthropocosmic trajectory is real, but hidden. It is not yet fully waxed, but eschatological.[53] The ugŭmch'i phenomenon renders *ki* (*pneuma*) as a significant hermeneutical key, which introduces a pneumatoanthropocosmic vision. *Ki*, a holistic and embracing term, signifies both the spiritual power and its material manifestation, and both the source of primordial *ki* and the medium of its empowerment.

The pneumatoanthropocosmic vision can cultivate a symbiosis of the life network through the communication of *ki* which fosters the human race's relationship with other lives more holistically and profoundly.

Furthermore, this vision invites us to thematize the *sociocosmic biography of the exploited life*, creatively pushing beyond the dialectical sociobiography of minjung and the innocent anthropocosmic vision.[54] Theotao tells the story of the sociocosmic network of the exploited life constituted by the spiritual communion of *ki* whose primordial *ki* is salvific, both emancipatory and reconcilatory. The ugŭmch'i phenomenon is an example of the sociocosmic biography of the exploited life, metaphorically telling the story of the two exploited lives, the feeble fishes in the turbulent stream and the multitude of minjung in the Ugŭmch'i War. In addition, *ki* as both spirit and matter can be a clue to solve the problem of incarnation. The birth story of Jesus depicts the pneumatoanthropocosmic vision *par excellence*, and the passion narratives of Christ tell the sociocosmic biography of the exploited life *par excellence*. Therefore, Jesus Christ as the theanthropocosmic Tao entails the *serendipitous pneumatosociocosmic trajectory* in the life-giving spirit of the primordial *ki*.

Since the pneumatic hermeneutics of *ki* and the sociocosmic biography of the exploited life are its constitutive parts, christotao (Christ as the Tao, the serendipitous pneumatosociocosmic trajectory) is a spiritual and emancipatory christology. Hence, christotao (Christ as the New *T'aegŭk*) is a paradigm of emancipatory christology embodied in the soteriological nucleus of Asian spirituality. That is to say, christotao (Jesus as the theanthropocosmic Tao) is an appropriate solution to the *koan* of this paper, overcoming modern historicism and Western dualism, the two basic problems of the contemporary christological impasse.

6. The Coming of *Yin* Christ

Christ as the New *T'aegŭk* (both *yang* and *yin*) is both divine and human, male and female, personal and impersonal, individual and communal. Nonetheless, this description is erroneous if it falls again into an objective and abstract description of Christ as the old *T'aegŭk*. But christotao must involve a prophetic hermeneutics of the Tao of Jesus Christ as the New *T'aegŭk*--that is to say, a responsibility to expose the new manifestation of pneumatocosmogonic transformation, i.e., the great reversal of the Tao. Whereas the time of *yang* Christ is waning, the period of *yin* Christ is waxing! Griffiths affirmed:

> This may sound very paradoxical and unreal, but for centuries now the western world has been following the path of *Yang*—of the masculine, active, aggressive, rational, scientific mind—and has brought the world near destruction. It is time now to recover the path of *Yin*, of the feminine, passive, patient, intuitive and poetic mind. This is the path which the *Tao Te Ching* sets before us.[55]

Indeed, we are now witnessing a kairological moment of the great christological turning point. *I-ching* describes: "After a time of decay comes the turning point. The powerful light that was banished returns. There is movement, but it is not brought about by force...thus the movement is natural, arising spontaneously...The old is discarded and the new is introduced."[56] There are already plenty of these natural and spontaneous signs for the coming of *Yin* Christ; for example, eco-feminist (sister), *sophia*, *Christo Mater*, *Christa*, female, Black and Asian womanist, liminal-marginal, and the second axial cosmic christologies.[57] The contemporary christological impasse is *de facto* an impasse of the white androcentric logos christologies, namely, the impasse of *yang Christ*. Those christologies are false and based on an ethnocentric myth whose demythologization provokes some emotional and awkward scholarship, the clear signs that they have reached their points of reversal. Remember that *T'aegŭk* has the subtle principle of reversal: When *yang* reaches its maximum intensity, it will revert to *yin*. Hence, in fact, this is a most creative moment for the interpretation of Jesus Christ. Whereas those "masculine, expansive, demanding, aggressive, competitive, rational, analytic" *yang* ('old') christologies are 'decarded,' "feminine, contractive, conservative, responsive, cooperative, intuitive, synthesizing" *yin* ('new') christotaos are 'introduced.'[58] The contrast between the *yang* christology and the *yin* christotao can be characterized as follows:[59]

Yin ←	*Yang*	*Yin* ←	*Yang*
tao	logos/praxis	feminine	masculine
christotao	christology/ christopraxis	uterine (womb)	phallo
intuitive (contemplative)	analytic (rational)	wholistic	dualistic
apophatic (kenotic)	kataphatic (phonocentric)	mutuality	domination
circular (cyclical)	linear (historical)	receptivity	violence
wu-wei (non-action action)	*yu-wei* (action action)		

Christ as Mystical-Prophetic Female

In the coming ages, Jesus as the Tao will be the mystical female, the cosmic womb. Christ as the New *T'aegŭk* will be the prophetic cosmogonic energy. And Jesus Christ will be the "Mystical-Prophetic" Female who embraces and heals the sociocosmic trajectory of the exploited life in her great bosom.[60] Christ the Tao will overcome the cosmic violence with her mysterious power of *wu-wei* (non-action action), with her paradoxical power of weakness and emptiness (according to

Graham, 'the preferential option to the strategy of *yin*'), and with her revolutionary power of the return.⁶¹ *Tao-te ching* states, "In Tao the only motion is returning; The only useful quality, weakness. For though Heaven and Earth and the Ten thousand Creatures were produced by Being, Being was produced by Non-being" (40). The ugŭmch'i phenomenon is a metaphorical example of these mysterious, paradoxical, revolutionary, and radical powers of return. The return of fish introduces a simple sign for the Great Return of the Mystical-Prophetic Female (the Tao) with the cosmogonic breathing of the Primordial *Ki*.

The millennial crusade of the patriarchal, hegemonic (kataphatic), phallo-onto-christology with the Western face of the *yang* (masculine) Viking-Rambo Jesus is now waning; a millennial march of the matrilineal, kenotic (apophatic), uterine-sapiential-christotao in the Asian heart of the *yin* (feminine) Sage Christ is rising. Through great non-action action in her uterine tranquility and sociocosmic serenity, Christ as the Mystical-Prophetic Female will heal this fragmented, divided, world torn down by the aggressive lynching of incarnated macho images, and will recover the harmonious wholeness through a radical return to the pneumatosociocosmic trajectory. The revolutionary non-action action is the dynamic spiritual upward movement of life against the apocalyptically disastrous downstream of history. Christ will dance not just an innocent cosmic dance but a revolutionary pneumatosociocosmic dance of life reverting upward against and transforming the vicious downstream of gloomy history together with (*perichoresis*) the feeble fishes in the polluted river (the exploited nature) and the minjung in Ugŭmch'i (the marginalized people).

Then, the task of Christian theology in the coming age will be the telling of the Tao of Jesus Christ, that is, the sociocosmic narrative of her and his pneumatic dancing with the exploited lives to transform the theanthropocosmic trajectory to the right path (so to speak, orthotao). Jesus Christ is the New *T'aegŭk* who has completed and generates the cosmogonic paradigm shift through crucifixion and resurrection. Christ as the theanthropocosmic Tao is also the outpouring primordial *ki*, the life-generating Energy-Spirit who empowers of the exploited lives to return to the serendipitous pneumatosociocosmic trajectory.

Chuang-tzu had Confucius saying: "*Ki* is empty and waits for the external things. Only the Tao gathers in emptiness. The cause of emptiness is the fasting of the mind-and-heart" (4). After all, Christ the Tao directs us to 'return' to the Tao, like the fish of the ŭmch'i phenomenon, in the radical power of emptiness (*kenosis*) and reversal (the Sermon on the Mount), through the fasting of the mind-and-heart (*metanoia*), under the direction of the Spirit (*sin-ki*). And Jesus said to Simon and Andrew: "Follow me and I will make you fish for people" (Mk. 1:17).[62]

Notes

[1] Burton Watson, trans., *The Complete Works Of Chuang Tzu* (New York and London: Columbia University Press, 1968), 302.

[2] See Albert Schweitzer, The Quest of the Historical Jesus: A Critical Study of its Progress from Reimarus to Wrede (New York: Macmillan, 1968); Rudoph Bultmann, History of the Synoptic Tradition (New York: Harper & Row, 1976); Günther Bornkmamm, Jesus of Nazareth, rev. ed. (Minneapolis: Fortress, 1995); John Dominic Crossan, The Historical Jesus: The Life of a Mediterranean Jewish Peasant (San Francisco: HaperCollins, 1994); and Marcus J. Borg, Jesus in Contemporary Scholarship (Valley Forge, PA: Trinity Press International, 1994).

[3] For an analysis of the myth of history, see Raimundo Panikkar, *Cosmotheandric Experience: Emerging Religious Consciousness* (Maryknoll: Orbis, 1993), 79-134.

[4] Root-metaphors denote the central metaphors such as logos and praxis that have shaped and governed narrative structures, cultural-linguistic matrices, or paradigms of theology and christology in wider definitions. The terms theology (theos + logos) and christology (christ + logos) were formulated in the process when the ancient Christian Church borrowed the logos from Greek philosophy and adopted it as the root-metaphor in their understanding of God and Christ.

[5] For more on this theme, see Chapter 5.

[6] This dualism is comparable to the distinction between a christology "from the above" and a christology "from the below;" see Wolfhart Pannenberg, *Jesus--God and Man,* trans. Lewis Wilkins and Duane Priebe (Philadelphia: Westminster, 1974),

33-7. For christopraxes of Latin American liberation theology, see Leonard Boff, *Jesus Christ Liberator: A Critical Christology for Our Time*, trans. Patrick Hughes (Maryknoll: Orbis, 1991); Jon Sobrino, *Jesus The Liberator: A Historical-Theological View*, trans. Paul Burns and Francis (Maryknoll: Orbis, 1993). For Occidental christopraxes, Tom F. Driver, *Christ in a Coming World: Toward an Ethical Christology* (New York: Crossroad, 1981); Jans Glebe-Möller, *Jesus and Theology: Critiques of a Tradition*, trans. Thor Hall (Minneapolis: Fortress, 1989); and Edmund Arens, *Christopraxis: A Theology of Action*, trans. John Hoffmeyer (Minneapolis: Fortress, 1995).

[7] Neo-Confucianism had developed this vision of the 'cosmic togetherness' in an organismic unity with Heaven, Earth, and the myriad things, as well expressed in the following passage of Chang Tsai's *Western Inscription*: "Heaven is my father and Earth is my mother, and even such a small creature as I find an intimate place in their midst. Therefore that which fills the universe I regard as my body and that which directs the universe I consider as my nature. All people are my brothers and sisters, and all things are my companions." (Chan Wing-tsit, trans., *A Source Book in Chinese Philosophy* [Princeton, NJ: Princeton University Press, 1963], 497-8). Also see Tu Wei-ming, *Centrality and Commonality: An Essay on Confucian Religiousness*, rev. ed. (Albany, NY: SUNY Press, 1989), 102-7.

[8] M. M. Thomas, *The Acknowledged Christ for the Indian Renaissance* (London: SCM, 1969); also R. Panikkar, *The Unknown Christ of Hinduism*, rev. ed. (Maryknoll: Orbis, 1964).

[9] For a version of minjung christology, see C. S. Song, *Jesus, The Crucified People* (New York: Crossroad, 1990). For a (Confucian) sage christology, see Heup Young Kim, *Wang Yang-ming and Karl Barth: A Confucian-Christian Dialogue* (Durham: University Press of America, 1996), 180-88; also M. Thomas Thangaraj, *The Crucified Guru: An Experiment in Cross-Cultural Christology* (Nashville: Abingdon, 1994). For a (Buddhist) bodhisattva christology, see Keel Hee-sung, "Jesus the Bodhisattva: Christology from a Buddhist Perspective," *Buddhist-Christian Studies* 16 (1996), 169-85; John P. Keenan, *The Meaning of Christ: A Mahayana Theology* (Maryknoll: Orbis, 1993); also Donald S. Lopez and Steven C. Rockfeller ed., *The Christ and The Bodhisattva* (Albany: SUNY Press, 1987).

[10] The Jesus Seminar seems to be a scholarly movement initiated by those who, epistemologically shocked by the destruction of their innocent image of the ethnocentric Christ through historical-critical study, have substituted a faith in scientific history for that ethnocentrically controlled Christian faith. Cf. Luke Timothy Johnson, *The Real Jesus: The Misguided Quest for the Historical Jesus and the Truth of the Traditional Gospels* (San Francisco: HarperSanFrancisco, 1996); also N. T. Wright, *Jesus and the Victory of God* (Minneapolis: Fortress, 1996).

[11] As the widely used root-metaphor of all classical East Asian religions including Confucianism, Taoism, and Buddhism, tao is a very inclusive term with various meanings. For example, a Confucian definition: "Tao is a Way, a path, a road, and by common metaphorical extension it becomes in ancient China the right Way of life, the Way of governing, the ideal Way of human existence, the Way of the Cosmos, the generative-normative Way (Pattern, path, course) of existence as such" (Herbert Fingarette, *Confucius—The Secular as Sacred* [New York: Harper & Row, 1972], 19). Tao also can be interpreted as "the logos in praxis" or "a being in becoming," as its Chinese character consists of two graphs meaning a head and a

movement ("to run"); see Wing-tsit Chan, *The Way of Lao Tzu: Tao-te ching* (Indianapolis & New York: Bobbs-Merrill, 1963), 6-10.

[12] The comparison among the three theological and christological paradigms based on the three root-metaphors can be illustrated as follows:

Root-metaphor	Theology	Christology	Metaphor	Character	Objective
logos	theo-logy	christo-logy	faith	understanding (doctrine)	orthodoxy
praxis	theo-praxis	christo-praxis	hope	action (ideology)	orthopraxis
tao	theo-tao	christo-tao	love	living (the way of life)	orthotao

[13] It is worth noting that the term logos does not appear in *The Gospel of Thomas*; see Stevan L. Davies, *The Gospel of Thomas and Christian Wisdom* (New York: Seabury, 1983), 81.

[14] See Marcus J. Borg, *Jesus*, esp., "Portraits of Jesus in Contemporary North American Scholarship," 18-43; also see Ben Witherington III, *Jesus the Sage: The Pilgrimage of Wisdom* (Minneapolis: Fortress, 1994). In addition, Bernard Lee analyzed the metaphors used for Jesus in the New Testament and proposed "a new development of a *Ruach/Dabhar* christology" to prevent ethnic violation (against the Jewishness of Jesus) and free from the metaphysical captivity of the logos christology; see his *Jesus and The Metaphors of God: The Christs of the New Testament* (New York: Paulist, 1993), 189.

[15] J. Moltmann, *The Way of Jesus Christ: Christology in Messianic Dimensions*, trans. Margaret Kohl (San Francisco: HarperSanFrancisco, 1990), xv; xiv.

[16] See A.. Pieris, Love Meets Wisdom: A Christian Experience of Buddhism (Maryknoll: Orbis, 1988); also An Asian Theology of Liberation (Maryknoll: Orbis, 1988).

[17] A. Pieris, *Fire and Water: Basic Issues in Asian Buddhism and Christianity* (Maryknoll: Orbis, 1996), esp., 146; also see 138-46. I appreciate Tissa Balassuriya for his introducing this article to me at the First Congress of Asian Theologians, May 1997, Suwon, Korea.

[18] See Fritjof Capra, The Tao of Physics: An Exploration of the Parallels Between Modern Physics and Eastern Mysticism, 3rd ed. (Boston: Shambhala, 1991), 11.

[19] For minjung theology, see Kim Yong-bock, ed., *Minjung Theology: People as Subjects of History*, rev. ed. (Singapore: The Christian Conference of Asia, 1981).

[20] Kim Chi Ha, *Sangmyung* (Seoul: Sol, 1992), 188-92. For a full English translation, see Chapter 5.

[21] This term *sin-ki* (Korean transliteration) is composed of two Chinese characters *shen-ch'i*. The first character *sin* (*shen*) has various translations such as ghost, spirit, soul, vitality, and sacred. The second character *ki*, well known in the Chinese term *ch'i*, is very similar to the Greek word *pneuma* and has also various translations such as energy, vital force, material force, and breath. For the following Chinese terms, in this paper, I use their Korean transliterations to preserve peculiar nuances in their Korean usage:

Chinese	ch'i	shen-ch'i	T'ai-chi	Wu-chi
Korean	ki	sin-ki	T'aegŭk	Mugŭk
translation	energy	vital energy	Great Ultimate	Non-Ultimate

[22] The last and fiercest battle during the second uprising of Tonghak peasant revolution which broke out on the Ugŭmch'i Hill of Gongju, Korea, in December of 1894.

[23] The definition of Suh Nam-dong, a founder of minjung theology in his *Minjung Theology*, 65. Suh's theology of *han* was heavily influenced by Chi Ha's philosophy of *han*.

[24] See Johann Baptist Metz, *Faith in History and Society: Toward a Practical Fundamental Theology*, trans. David Smith (New York: Seabury, 1980).

[25] See Chung Hyun Kyung, "*Han-pu-ri*: Doing Theology from Korean Women's Perspective," *The Ecumenical Reviews* 40:1 (1988), 27-36.

[26] The last dynasty of Korea (1392-1910).

[27] For the pneumatoanthropocosmic vision, see my "Asian Theology," 285-7.

[28] Chan Wing-tsit, trans. and compiled, *A Source Book in Chinese Philosophy* (Princeton, NJ.: Princeton University Press, 1963), 463.

[29] Jaroslav Pelikan, *Jesus Through the Centuries: His Place in the History of Culture* (New York: Harper & Row, 1985), 58. For the cosmic Christ in the Bible and Christian traditions, also see Matthew Fox, *The Coming of the Cosmic Christ: The Healing of Mother Earth and the Birth of a Global Consciousness* (San Francisco: Harper & Row, 1988), esp., 75-128.

[30] Translation from Thomas Merton, *Thoughts on The East* (New York: New Directions Publishing, 1995), 25-6. For general introduction to the tao, see Max Kaltenmark, *Lao Tzu and Taoism*, trans. Roger Greaves (Stanford: Stanford University Press, 1969); also A. C. Graham, *Disputers of the Tao: Philosophical Argument in Ancient China* (La Salle, IL.: Open Court, 1989). For Chuang-tzu's understanding of the tao, see Chad Hansen, "A Tao of Tao in Chuang-tzu," *Experimental Essays on Chuang-tzu*, ed. by Victor H. Mair (Hawaii: University of Hawaii Press, 1983), 24-55; Philip J. Ivanhoe, "Zhuangzi on Skepticism, Skill, and the Ineffable *Dao*," *Journal of American Academy of Religion* 91:4 (1993), 639-53. For comparative studies between tao and logos, see Zhang Longxi, *The Tao and the Logos: Literary Hermeneutics, East and West* (Durham & London: Duke University Press, 1992); Mark Berkson, "Language: The Guest of Reality—Zhuanzi and Derrida on Language, Reality, and Skillfulness," *Essays on Skepticism, Relativism, and Ethics in the Zhuangzi*, ed. by Paul Kjellberg and Philip J. Ivanhoe (Albany, NY: SUNY Press, 1996), 97-126; James W. Stines, "I Am The Way: Michael Polany's Taoism," *Zygon* 20:1 (1995), 59-77.

[31] Translation from Chan, *Source Book*, 139; cf. *The Sophia of Jesus Christ:* 94.

[32] Chan, *Source Book*, 144.

[33] Graham, *Disputers*, 223.

[34] Chan, *Source Book*, 147.

[35] Bede Griffiths, selected and introduced, *Universal Wisdom: A Journey Through the Sacred Wisdom of the World* (San Francisco: HarperSanfrancisco, 1994), 27.

[36] For a general introduction to Taoism, see Liu Xiaogan, "Taoism," *Our Religions*, ed. by Arvind Sharma (San Francisco: HarperSanFrancisco, 1993), 229-89; for Confucianism, see Tu Wei-ming, "Confucianism," ibid., 139-227.

[37] Jean Sangbae Ri, Confucius et Jesus Christ: La Premiere Theologie Chretinnene en Coree D'apres L'oeurvre de Yi Piek lettre Confuceen 1754-1786 (Paris: Editions Beauchesne, 1979).

[38] Etymologically, tao also denotes a beginning at the crossroads.

[39] Kim Heung-ho, "Ryu Young-mo's View of Christianity from the Asian perspective," Park Young-ho, ed., *Tasŏk Ryu Young-mo* (Seoul: Muae, 1993), 299.

[40] By this Korean word, Ryu expressed two metaphorical meanings of the cross simultaneously. On the cross, Jesus spilled blood like the blood of flower, which is also like the blossoming of the flower (of life).

[41] Kim Heung-ho, "Ryu Young-mo's View," 301.

[42] Kim Heung-ho, *Chesori* [The Genuine Voice: The Words of Ryu Young-mo] (Seoul: Pungman, 1985), 68.

[43] Lee Jung Yong, The Theology of Change: A Christian Concept of God in an Eastern Perspective (Maryknoll: Orbis, 1979), 11-28.

[44] Ibid., 20.

[45] Wilfred Cantwell Smith, *Faith of Other Men* (New York: New American Library, 1963), 72.

[46] Lee, *Change*, 22.

[47] Ibid., 99.

[48] See Lee Jung Young, *The Trinity In Asian Perspective* (Nashville: Abingdon, 1996), pp.78-82.

[49] As a composite adjective of *theos* (God), *anthropos* (humanity), and *cosmos* (universe), literally, theanthropocosmic refers to the interrelation of God, humanity, and the cosmos. It is comparable to the cosmotheandrism of Raimundo Panikkar; see his *Cosmotheandric Experience*; also *The Trinity and the Religious Experience of Man* (New York: Orbis, 1973). But my position comes from my experiences of the concrete context where the fusion of horizons has been in progress between the two great traditions; namely the anthropo-cosmic paradigm of Neo-Confucianism and the theo-historical paradigm of Christianity. For this, see my *Wang Yang-ming and Karl Barth*, esp., 175-88.

[50] For a comparative study with tao, see Holmes Welch, *The Parting the Way: Lao Tzu and the Taoist Movement* (Boston: Beacon, 1957), esp., 50-82. For Christian mystical traditions including Hildegrad of Bingden (1098-1179), Bonaventura (1221-74), and Dante Alighieri (1265-1321), see Ewert H. Cousins, *Christ of the 21st Century* (Rockport, MA.: Element, 1992); also Fox, *Cosmic Christ*, 109-26. For an introduction to Nicholas of Cusa, Karl Jaspers, *The Great Philosophers: The Original Thinkers*, trans. Ralph Manheim (New York: Harcourt, Brace & World, Inc., 1966), 116-272. For Julian of Norwich, see Brant Pelphrey, *Christ Our Mother: Julian of Norwich* (Wilmington: Michael Glaizer, 1989).

[51] The understanding of logos has been modified and developed notably since Western christologies adopted it as their root-metaphor. The similar fusion of hermeneutical horizons will evolve in the process of making a christotao. Tao also need to adapt and change partly when East Asian Christians articulate their faith in Jesus Christ. A formulation here demonstrates an example of the modification.

[52] I borrowed this expression from Gordon D. Kaufman, though I do not fully agree with his vision of the cosmic evolutionary-historical trajectory which still is more or less linear, pragmatist, and historicist. See his *In Face of Mystery: A Constructive Theology* (Cambridge, MA.: Harvard University Press, 1993), 264-80.

⁵³ In this *T'aegŭk* christology, eschatology is conceived as the other side of history; for example, if history refers to the visible part of the moon, eschatology signifies its invisible part.

⁵⁴ Kim Yong-bock argued that the social biography of minjung is a more authentic historical point of reference for theological reflection than the doctrinal discourses superimposed by the Church and in the orientation of Western rationality; see his "Theology and the Social Biography of Minjung," *CTC Bulletin:* 5:3-6:1 (1984-5), 66-78. For the sociocosmic narrative of the exploited life, see my "Asian Theology," 285-90.

⁵⁵ Griffiths, *Universal Wisdom,* 27-8.

⁵⁶ Richard Wilhelm, trans., *The I Ching or Book of Changes,* 3rd ed. (Princeton, NJ: Princeton University Press, 1967), 97.

⁵⁷ For example, Rosemary Radford Ruether, *Sexism and God-Talk: Toward a Feminist Theology* (Boston: Beacon, 1983), 116-38; Elizabeth Schüssler Fiorenza, *Jesus: Miriam's Child, Sophia's Prophet, Critical Issues in Feminist Christology* (New York: Continuum, 1995); Mark Kline Taylor, *Remembering Esperanza: A Cultural-Political Theology for North American Praxis* (Maryknoll: Orbis, 1990), 194-245; Julie M. Hopkins, *Towards A Feminist Christology: Jesus of Nazareth, European Women, and the Christological Crisis* (Grand Rapids: Eerdmans, 1994), 81-97; Rita Nakashima Brock, *Journey by Heart: A Christology of Erotic Power* (New York: Crossroad, 1983); Rose Horman Arthur, *The Wisdom Goddess: Feminine Motifs in Eight Nag Hammadi Documents* (Lanham: University Press of America, 1984); Jacquelyn Grant, *Black Women's Jesus, White Women's Christ* (Atlanta: Scholars, 1985); Chung Hyun Kyung, "Who is Jesus for Asian Women?" in *Asian Faces of Jesus,* ed. by R.S. Sugirtharajah (Maryknoll: Orbis, 1993), 223-46; Majella Franzmann, *Jesus in the Nag Hammadi Writings* (Edinburgh: T&T Clark, 1996); Lee Jung Young, *Marginality: The Key to Multicultural Theology* (Minneapolis: Fortress, 1995); Cousins, *Christ*; and Fox, *Cosmic Christ.*

⁵⁸ Fritzof Capra, *The Turning Point: Science, Society, and the Rising Culture* (Toronto: Bantam Books, 1982), 37-8. For the need of the transformation of Western culture, see ibid., 21-49.

⁵⁹ These characterizations do not connote an essentialism (related to an Aristotelian theory of sexuality) but a "dynamic balance," as Capra clarified well (see ibid., 35-7). Thus I reject both the patriarchal and the feminist biases in the association of *yin.* Christotao is thematized in the context of the Great Ultimate (the Change) which transcends both substantialism (being) and processism (becoming), identifying the reality as the constant change. It is no longer related to a mutually exclusive choice of sexuality between female and male (the Western logic of either-or), but to the mutually inclusive relationship not only between male and female but also between personal and impersonal (the Asian mode of both-and). In this paradigm of the complementary opposites, "nothing is only *yin* or only *yang.*" Simply, they refer to a responsible hermeneutics for the dynamic balance of the serendipitous pneumatosociocosmic trajectory at a given time (as *I-Ching* reads a hexagram pertinent to a historical context).

As Richard Wilhelm clarified, these characterizations do not refer to objective representations of entities as such but of their functional tendencies in movement (see Wilhelm, *I-ching,* p l.). As Karl Jüng observed, this hermeneutics is not related to the chain process of causality (the prime logic of Western science and philosophy) but to what he calls "synchronicity" that "takes the coincidence of events in space and time as meaning something more than mere chance, namely, a peculiar interdependence of objective events among themselves as well as with the subjective states of the observer or observers" (ibid., xxiv).

[60] I borrowed this composite adjective from David Tracy; see his *Dialogue With The Other: The Inter-religious Dialogue* (Louvain: Peeters, 1990), 7.

[61] Jesus used the principle of reversal masterfully, as he said, "Whoever wants to be first must be last of all" (Mk. 9:35) or "For those who want to save their life will lose it, and those who lose their life for my sake will find it" (Mt. 16:25). Furthermore, he stated in the Sermon on the Mount:

"Blessed are you who are poor, for yours is the kingdom of God. Blessed are you who are hungry now, for you will be filled. Blessed are you who weep now, for you will laugh. Blessed are you when people hate you. . . . Rejoice in that day . . . . But woe to you who are rich, for you have received your consolation. Woe to you who are full now, for you will be hungry. Woe to you who are laughing now, for you will mourn and weep. . . . do good to those who hate you, bless those who curse you, pray those who abuse you." (Lk. 6:20-28 NRSV)

[62] It is not unimportant to note that the pictogram of *T'aegŭk* (as in the national flag of South Korea) portrays the dancing of two fishes.

Glossary of Chinese (Korean) Terms

ai	love	愛
ch'eng	sincerity	誠
ch'eng-i	the sincerity of the will	誠意
cheng-hsin	the rectification of the mind-and-heart	正心
ch'i (ki)	material force, vital energy	氣
chih	knowledge	知
chih	wisdom	智
chih liang-chih	the extension of *liang-chih*	致良知
ch'in-min	loving people	親民
ching (kyŏng)	reverence, piety, mindfulness	敬
ch'ing	feeling	情
chung	equlibrium	中
Chung-yung	*The Doctrine of Means*	中庸
hsin	faithfulness	信
hsin	mind-and-heart	心
hsin chih li	the identity of mind-and-heart and principle	心卽理
hsing	Nature, human nature	性
hsing chi li	the identity of nature and principle	性卽理
I	*The Change*	易
i	righteousness	義
il-ki [*i-ch'i*]	primordial energy	一氣
jen	human being	人
jen	benevolence, co-humanity	仁
jen-hsin	the human mind	人心
ki [*ch'i*]	material force, vital energy	氣
ko-wu	the investigation of things	格物
kyŏng [*ching*]	reverence, piety, mindfulness	敬
li	principle	理
li	propriety	禮

liang-chih	the innate knowledge of the good	良知
liang-hsin	good conscience	良心
li-chih	the establishment of the will	立志
ming-te	the clear character	明德
Mugŭk [*wu-chi*]	the Non-Ultimate	無極
Shang-ti	the Lord on the High	上帝
shen	body	身
shen	Spirit, God	神
shu	reciprocity	恕
sin-ki [*shen-ch'i*]	vital energy	神氣
T'aegŭk [*T'ai-chi*]	the Great Ultimate	太極
T'ai-hsu	Great Vacuity	太虛
T'ai-chi (*T'aegŭk*)	the Great Ultimate	太極
Tao	the Way	道
Tao-hsin	the mind of Tao	道心
te	virtue	德
t'i	substance	體
T'ien-li	Heavenly Principle, Principle of Nature	天理
T'ien-ming	Heavenly Endowment, the Mandate of Heaven	天命
Wan-wu i-t'i	the Oneness of All Things	萬物一體
wu-wei	non-action action	無為
yang	yang	陽
yin	yin	陰
yüan, heng, li, chen	origination, flourshing, benefitting, firmness	元亨利貞
yung	function	用

Credits

Chapter 1 is adapted from a paper presented to the American Academy of Religion, San Francisco, November, 1992, previously published in *Asia Journal of Theology* 8:2 (1994) as "*Jen* and *Agape*: Toward a Confucian Christology."

Chapter 2 is adapted from a paper presented to the Third International Confucian-Christian Dialogue at the Boston University, Boston, August 25, 1994, previously published in *Korea Journal of Systematic Theology* (2001) as "*Liang-chih* and *Humanitas Christi*: an Encounter of Wang Yang-ming and Karl Barth."

Chapter 3 is adapted from a paper presented to the Fourth International Confucian-Christian Dialogue at the Chinese University of Hong Kong, Hong Kong, December 21, 1998, previously published as in *Ching Feng* 41: 3-4 (1998) as "*Imago Dei* and *T'ien-ming*: John Calvin and Yi T'oegye on Humanity."

Chapter 4 is adapted from an article originally published in *Third Millennium* 4:1 (2001) as "Owning up to Our Own Metaphors: A Christian Journey in the Neo-Confucian Wilderness." It was republished in *Visioning New Life Together Among Asian Religions: The Third Congress of Asian Theologians (CATS III),* ed. Daniel S. Thiagarajah and A Wati Longchar (Christian Conference of Asia, 2002), 243-253.

Chapter 5 is adapted from a paper to the First Congress of Asian Theologians at the Somang Academy, Suwon, Korea, May 27, 1997, previously published in *Asia Journal of Theology* 13:2 (1999) as "A Tao of Asian Theology in the Twenty First Century."

Chapter 6 is adapted from a paper presented to the Second Congress of Asian Theologians, Bangalore, India, Aug.12, 1999, previously published in *Studies in Interreligious Dialogue* 10:1 (2000) as "Toward a Christotao: Christ as the Theanthropocosmic Tao."

www.ingramcontent.com/pod-product-compliance
Lightning Source LLC
Chambersburg PA
CBHW072131160426
43197CB00012B/2063